Introduction

In today's ever-evolving world of social media, content creators are continually seeking tools to streamline their workflows and produce high-quality content. Recognizing these challenges, David Chapman, Kelvin Harris Jr., and Yaw Baidoo of On Our Own Media Group have curated this guide as a comprehensive resource for creators who want to save time while maximizing creativity.

This book is designed to empower creators at all levels—whether you're an influencer crafting your brand, a videographer building your portfolio, or someone venturing into content creation for the first time. With a focus on practical tools and proven strategies, these volumes provide insights into streamlining workflows, enhancing productivity, and creating content that truly resonates.

1. Anchor.fm

- **What it does:** Anchor.fm is a free podcast distribution platform that simplifies the process of recording, editing, and distributing podcasts across major platforms like Spotify and Apple Podcasts.

- **Resource type:** Podcast hosting and distribution.

- **Cost:** Free.

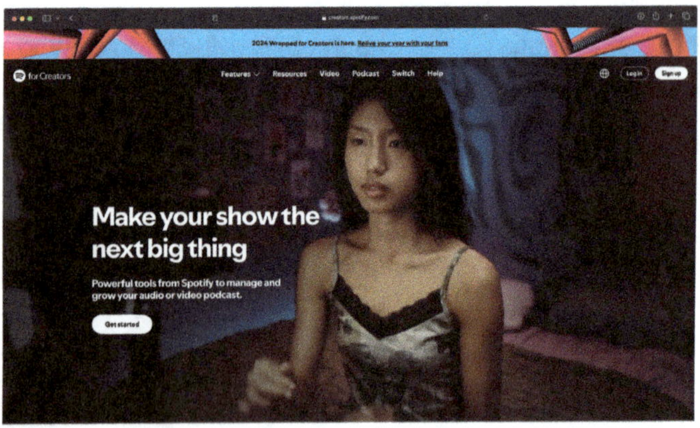

- **How it saves time:** By offering an all-in-one solution, Anchor.fm eliminates the need for multiple tools, allowing creators to manage their podcasting workflow seamlessly.

2. Artlist.io

- **What it does:** Artlist.io provides a vast library of high-quality, royalty-free music and sound effects suitable for various multimedia projects.

- **Resource type:** Music licensing platform.

- **Cost:** Subscription-based (various plans available).

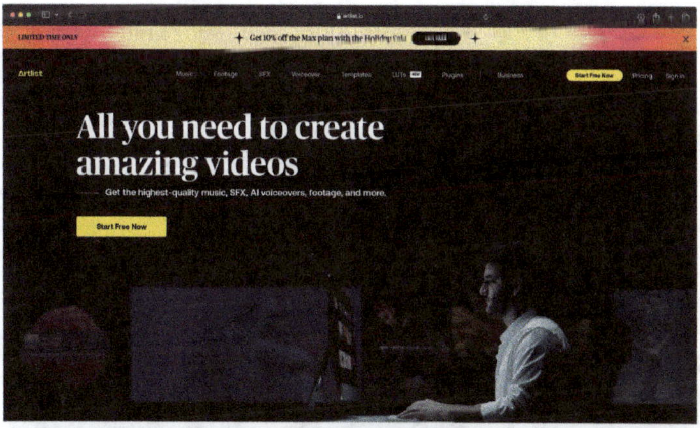

- **How it saves time:** With a user-friendly interface and extensive search capabilities, creators can quickly find and license the perfect track, streamlining the audio selection process.

3. Bubbl.us

- **What it does:** Bubbl.us is an online brainstorming tool that enables users to create mind maps and organize ideas visually.

- **Resource type:** Mind mapping and brainstorming application.

- **Cost:** Free with basic features; premium plans available.

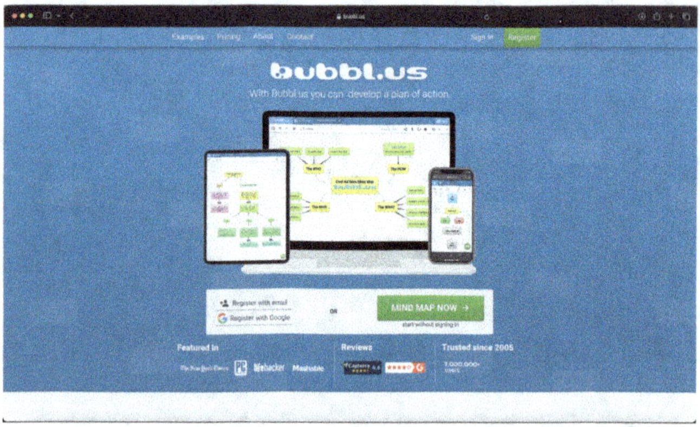

- **How it saves time:** Facilitates quick idea generation and organization, aiding in efficient project planning and content strategy development.

4. Contentdrips.com

- **What it does:** Contentdrips.com assists in creating branded video snippets and captions, enhancing social media content.

- **Resource type:** Content creation tool.

- **Cost:** Paid plans.

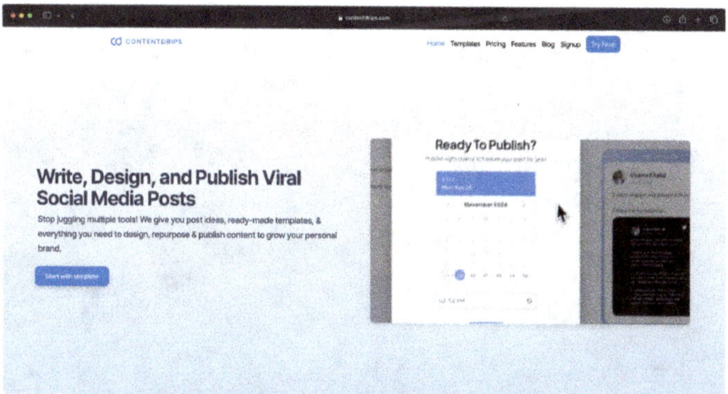

- **How it saves time:** Automates the creation of engaging video content, reducing manual editing efforts.

5. Flodesk.com

- **What it does:** Flodesk.com is an email marketing service that enables users to design and send visually appealing emails.

- **Resource type:** Email marketing platform.

- **Cost:** Paid plans.

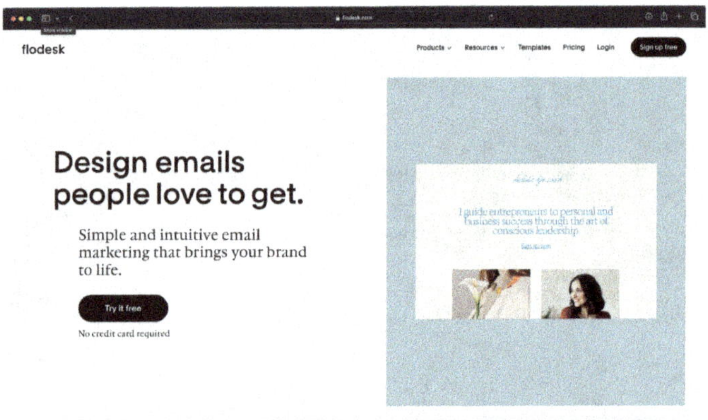

- **How it saves time:** Offers intuitive design tools and templates, simplifying the email creation process.

6. Hunter.io

- **What it does:** Hunter.io allows users to find and verify professional email addresses associated with any domain.

- **Resource type:** Email lookup and verification tool.

- **Cost:** Free tier available; premium plans for additional features.

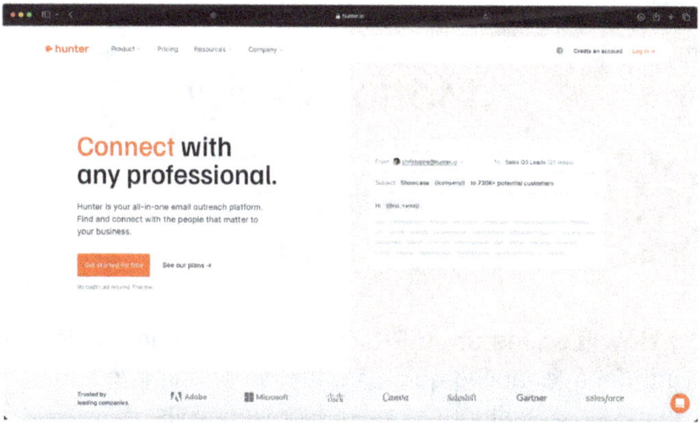

- **How it saves time:** Streamlines the process of finding contact information, facilitating efficient outreach efforts.

7. Jitter.video

- **What it does:** Jitter.video is an online tool for creating simple animations and motion designs.

- **Resource type:** Animation creation platform.

- **Cost:** Free with basic features; premium plans available.

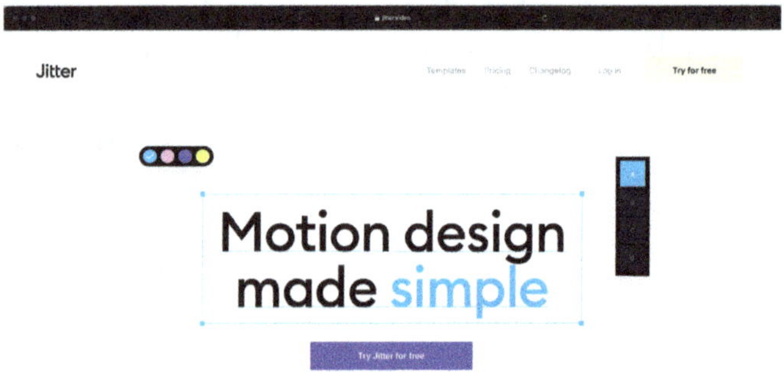

- **How it saves time:** Provides templates and an intuitive interface, enabling quick production of animated content without extensive design skills.

8. Kamua.com

- What it does: Kamua.com is an AI-powered video editing tool that automates the process of resizing and repurposing videos for various platforms.

- Resource type: Video editing and repurposing tool.

- **Cost:** Paid plans.

- **How it saves time:** Automates video formatting tasks, ensuring content fits platform specifications without manual adjustments.

9. Notion.so

- **What it does:** Notion.so is an all-in-one workspace that combines notes, tasks, databases, and calendars for seamless collaboration.

- **Resource type:** Productivity and collaboration platform.

- **Cost:** Free with basic features; premium plans available.

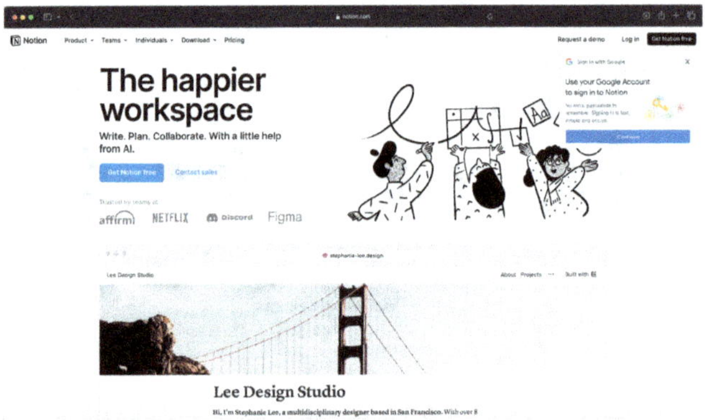

- **How it saves time:** Centralizes various work tools into one platform, reducing the need to switch between multiple applications.

10. Repurpose.io

- **What it does:** Repurpose.io automates the distribution of content from platforms like TikTok to other social media channels.

- **Resource type:** Content automation and marketing tool.

- **Cost:** Paid plans.

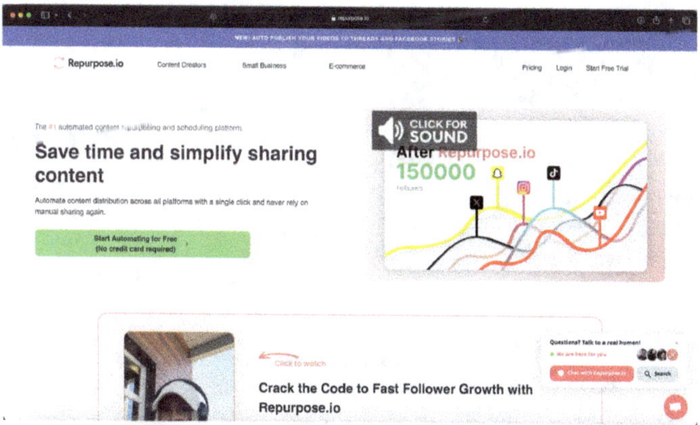

- **How it saves time:** Automates cross-platform content sharing, eliminating repetitive manual posting tasks.

11. Smallpdf.com

- **What it does:** Smallpdf.com simplifies PDF-related tasks such as compression, conversion, and editing.

- **Resource type:** Document management tool.

- **Cost:** Free tier available; premium plans for advanced features.

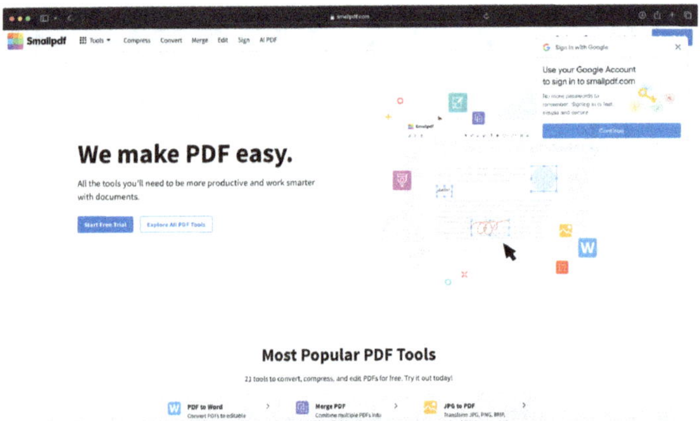

- **How it saves time:** Reduces the effort required to manage and edit PDF files, streamlining administrative tasks for creators.

12. Planoly.com

- **What it does:** Planoly.com is a social media management platform for planning and scheduling posts, especially on Instagram and Pinterest.

- **Resource type:** Social media scheduler.

- **Cost:** Free tier available; premium plans for additional features.

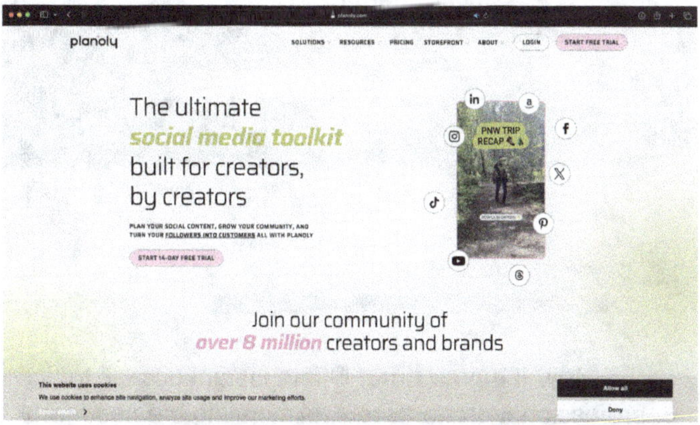

- **How it saves time:** Allows creators to schedule posts in advance and visually plan their feed, ensuring a cohesive aesthetic without daily posting efforts.

13. Storyblocks.com

- **What it does:** Storyblocks.com provides a library of royalty-free video, audio, and image assets for creators.

- **Resource type:** Stock media platform.

- **Cost:** Subscription-based plans.

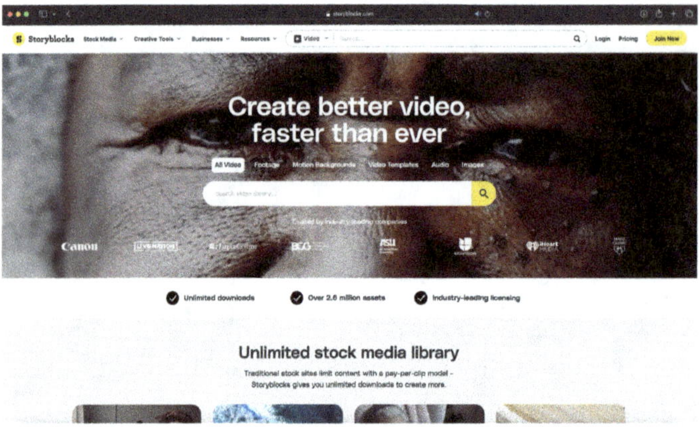

- **How it saves time:** Offers instant access to professional-grade assets, eliminating the need for time-consuming content creation.

14. Vidyo.ai

- **What it does:** Vidyo.ai converts long-form videos into short, engaging clips with captions optimized for social media.

- **Resource type:** Video editing automation tool.

- **Cost:** Free.

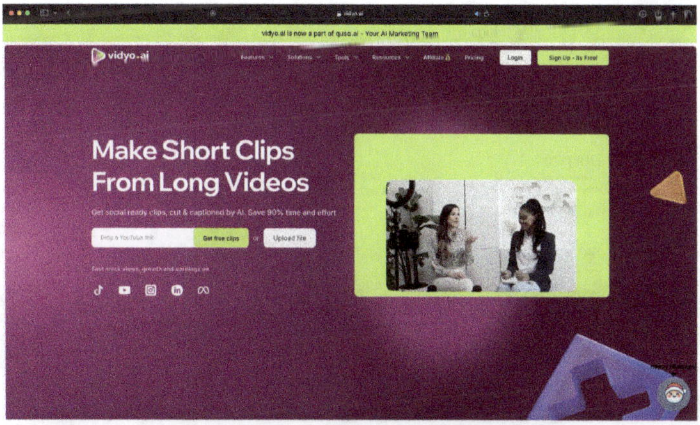

- **How it saves time:** Automates the process of creating short-form video content, enabling creators to quickly repurpose their existing material.

15. Unsplash.com

- **What it does:** Offers a vast collection of high-quality, royalty-free images for creators.

- **Resource type:** Stock photo library.

- **Cost:** Free.

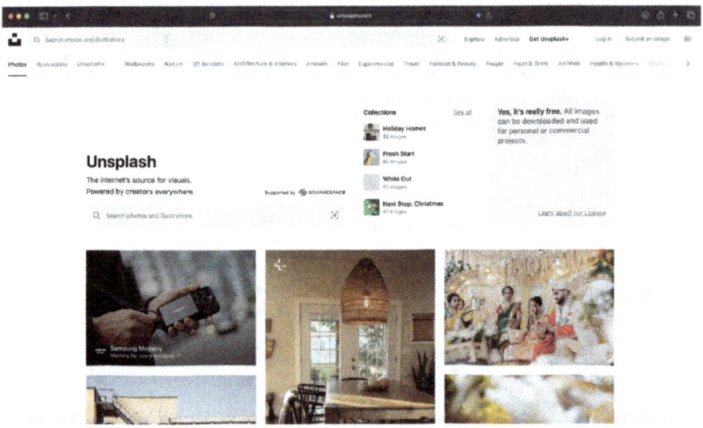

- **How it saves time:** Provides instant access to professional-quality visuals, reducing the need for photoshoots.

16. Trello.com

- **What it does:** Trello is a task management tool that organizes projects through boards, lists, and cards.

- **Resource type:** Project management tool.

- **Cost:** Free tier; premium plans for teams.

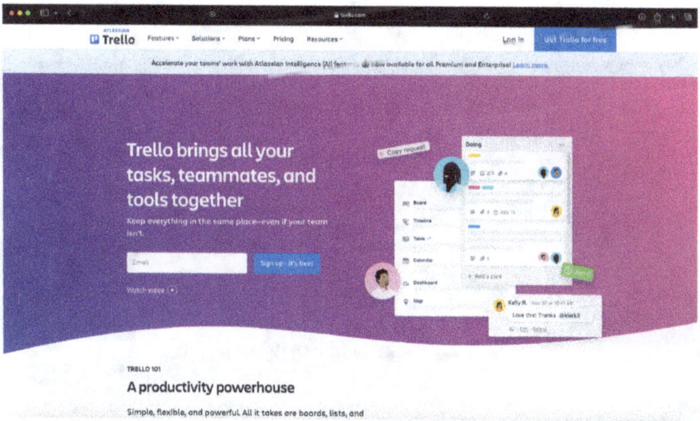

- **How it saves time:** Simplifies task tracking and team collaboration, improving productivity and project oversight.

17. Directtoconsumer.co

- **What it does:** Provides insights and strategies for direct-to-consumer (DTC) brands to optimize marketing and sales.
- **Resource type:** Marketing and branding tool.

- **Cost:** Free resources; paid services.

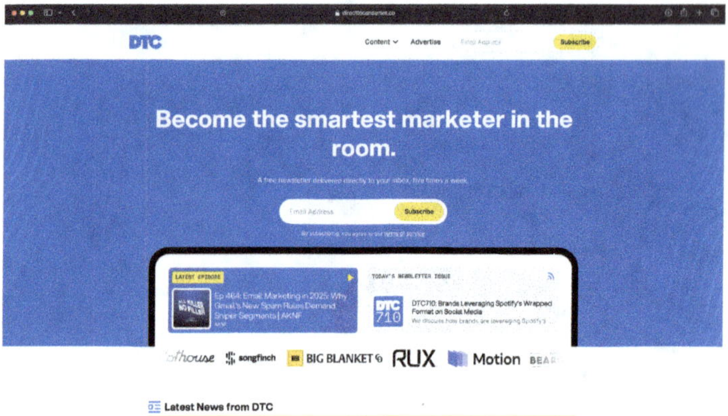

- **How it saves time:** Offers pre-built templates and guides for DTC campaigns, eliminating the guesswork in marketing strategy.

18. Similarweb.com

- **What it does:** Delivers analytics and insights into website traffic, rankings, and performance.

- **Resource type:** Website analytics platform.

- **Cost:** Free tier available; premium plans for in-depth insights.

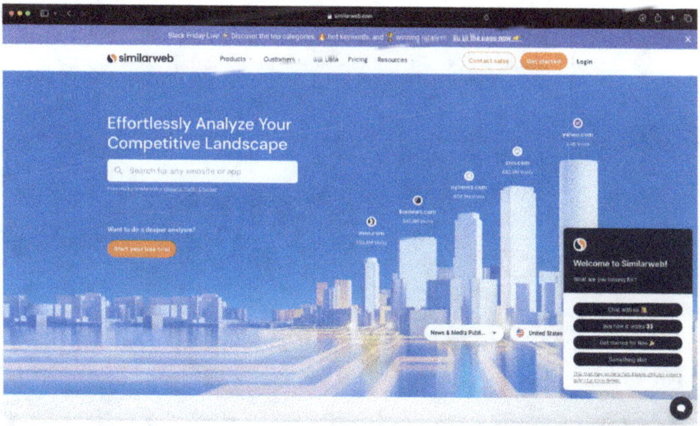

- **How it saves time:** Provides instant competitor analysis and website insights to inform marketing strategies.

19. Hubspot.com

- **What it does:** An all-in-one CRM platform offering tools for marketing, sales, and customer service.

- **Resource type:** CRM and marketing software.

- **Cost:** Free tier available; premium plans for advanced features.

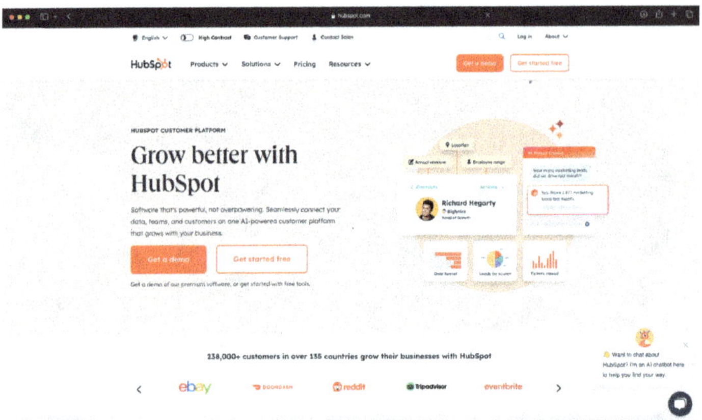

- **How it saves time:** Consolidates customer management tools into one platform, streamlining workflows.

20. Copy.ai

- **What it does:** AI-powered tool for generating marketing copy, emails, and social media content.

- **Resource type:** Content creation platform.

- **Cost:** Free trial available; paid plans for full access.

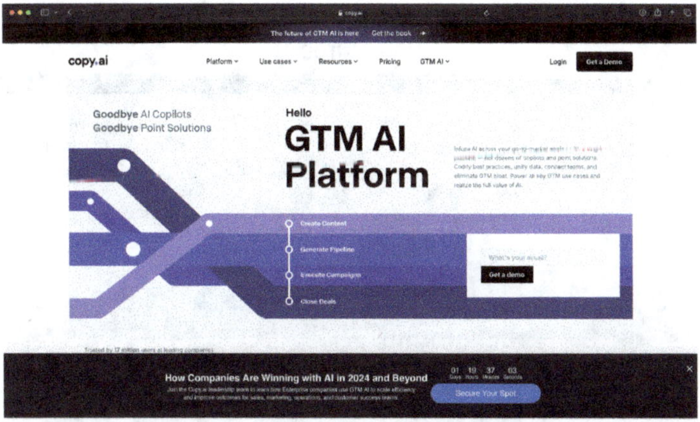

- **How it saves time:** Automates content writing, reducing the time spent on brainstorming and drafting.

21. Remove.bg

- **What it does:** Instantly removes backgrounds from images, leaving a clean subject.

- **Resource type:** Image editing tool.

- **Cost:** Free with limited downloads; paid for additional features.

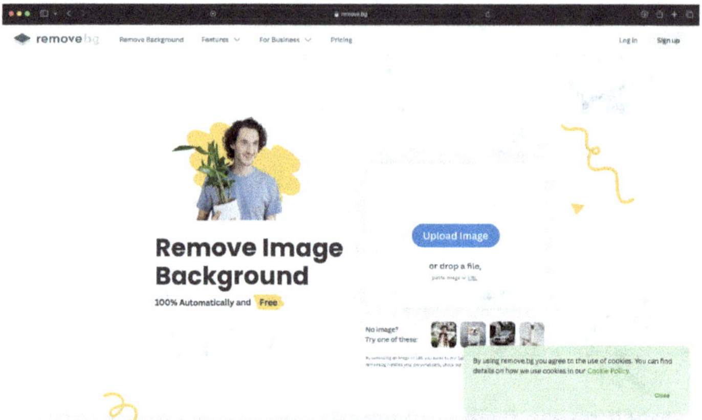

- **How it saves time:** Eliminates the need for manual background editing, providing fast, professional results.

22. AnswerThePublic.com

- **What it does:** Offers insights into search queries, providing content ideas based on what people are searching for.

- **Resource type:** Keyword and content research tool.

- **Cost:** Free limited searches; paid plans for more access.

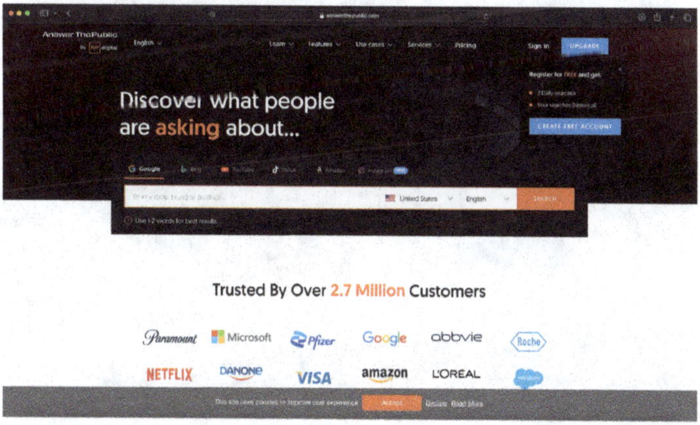

- **How it saves time:** Quickly generates content ideas, eliminating hours of manual research.

23. Snazzy.ai

- **What it does:** Uses AI to generate creative marketing copy, blogs, and ad texts.

- **Resource type:** Copywriting automation tool.

- **Cost:** Free trial available; paid plans for full features.

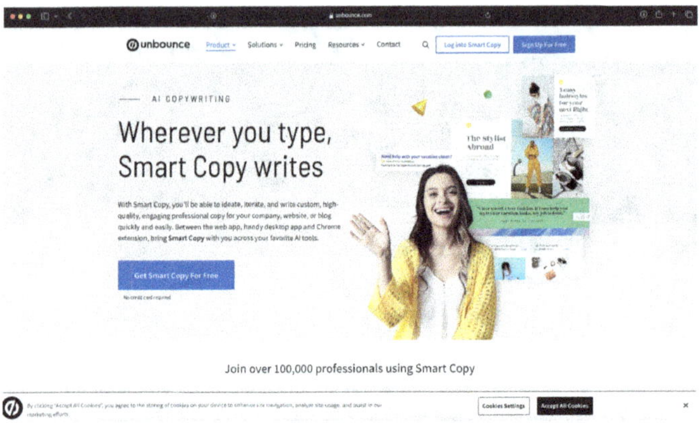

- **How it saves time:** Accelerates the content creation process with AI-driven suggestions.

24. Tailorbrands.com

- **What it does:** Helps create logos, websites, and branded materials for businesses.

- **Resource type:** Branding and design platform.

- **Cost:** Paid plans.

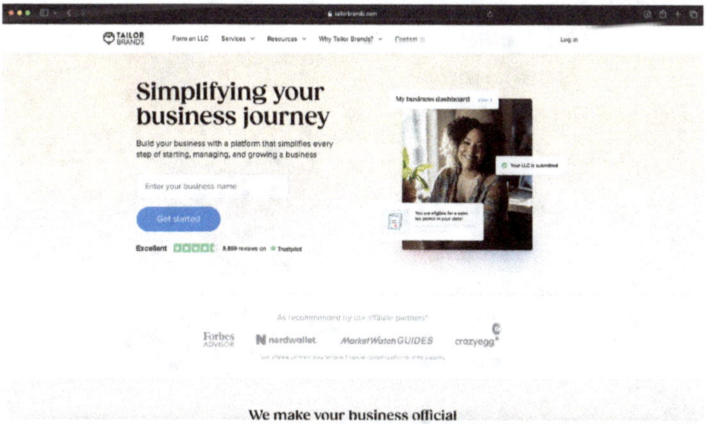

- **How it saves time:** Provides ready-made branding tools, eliminating the need to hire designers.

25. Pixelhunter.io

- **What it does:** Automatically resizes images to fit various social media platforms.

- **Resource type:** Image optimization tool.

- **Cost:** Free.

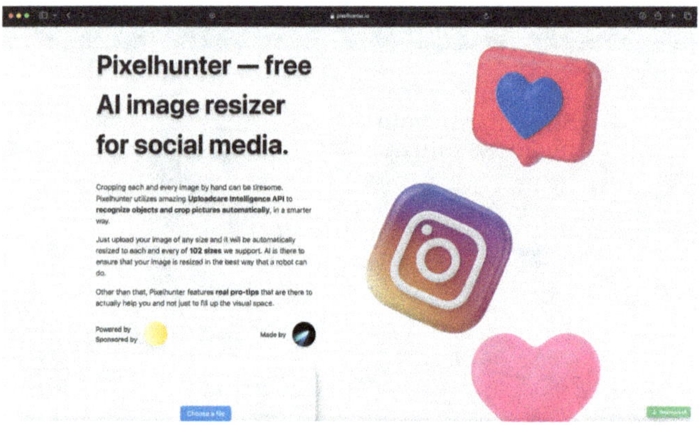

- **How it saves time:** Streamlines the process of adapting images to multiple platform specifications.

26. ReallyGoodEmails.com

- **What it does:** A curated collection of email designs for inspiration.

- **Resource type:** Design inspiration resource.

- **Cost:** Free.

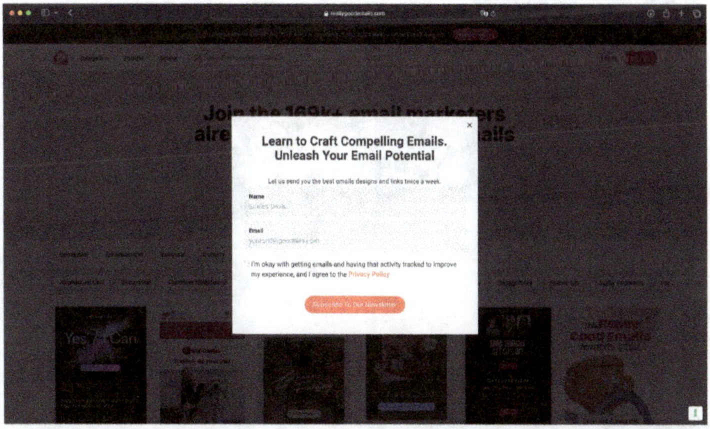

- **How it saves time:** Offers pre-built design examples, reducing the effort in conceptualizing email layouts.

27. Tiktokhashtags.com

- **What it does:** Provides trending and relevant hashtags for TikTok videos.

- **Resource type:** Hashtag research tool.

- **Cost:** Free.

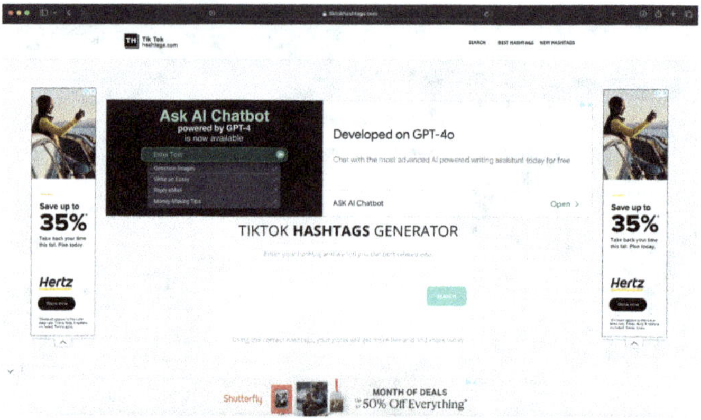

- **How it saves time:** Helps creators maximize reach by quickly finding effective hashtags.

28. SimilarTech.com

- **What it does:** Analyzes technology stacks used by websites.

- **Resource type:** Tech research platform.

- **Cost:** Free with limited features; paid plans available.

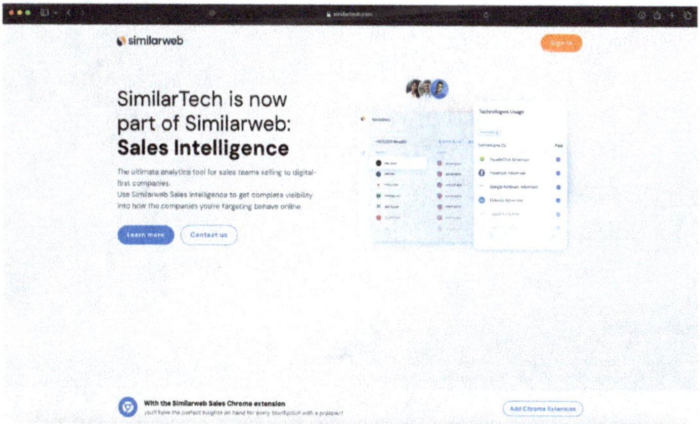

- **How it saves time:** Assists in understanding competitors' tech strategies efficiently.

29. Axiom.ai

- **What it does:** Automates repetitive browser tasks like data entry or scraping.

- **Resource type:** Automation tool.

- **Cost:** Free with basic features; premium plans available.

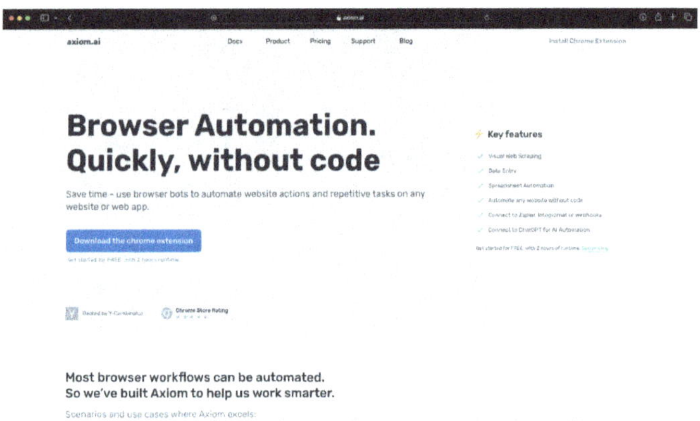

- **How it saves time:** Reduces manual browser tasks, freeing up time for creative work.

30. Crello.com

- **What it does:** A graphic design tool for creating social media posts, ads, and more.

- **Resource type:** Design platform.

- **Cost:** Free with basic features; paid plans for premium access.

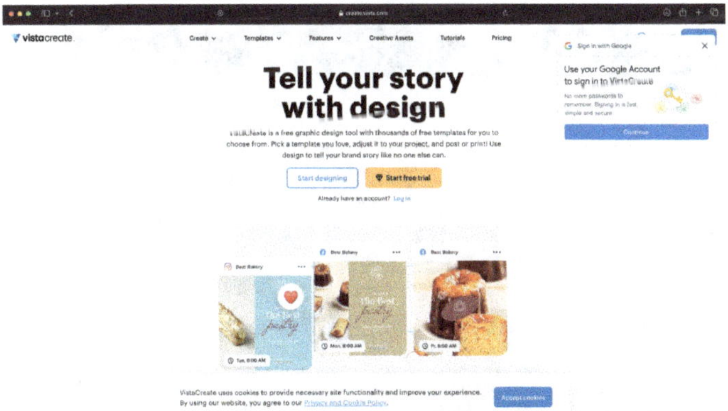

- **How it saves time:** Offers customizable templates, enabling quick creation of professional designs.

31. Synthesia.io

- **What it does:** AI tool for creating videos with virtual presenters.

- **Resource type:** AI video creation tool.

- **Cost:** Paid plans.

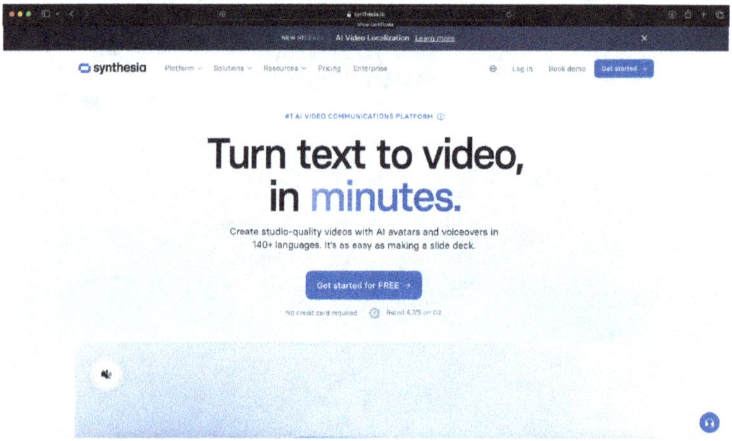

- **How it saves time:** Automates video production, allowing creators to generate professional content quickly.

32. ThinkWithGoogle.com

- **What it does:** Provides insights, tools, and case studies to improve marketing strategies.

- **Resource type:** Marketing research platform.

- **Cost:** Free.

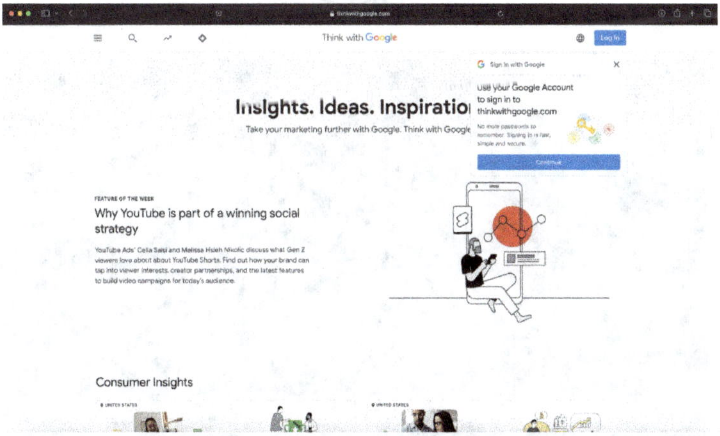

- **How it saves time:** Offers pre-researched data and trends, saving time on market analysis.

33. Unroll.me

- **What it does:** Helps manage email subscriptions by organizing and unsubscribing in bulk.

- **Resource type:** Email management tool.

- **Cost:** Free.

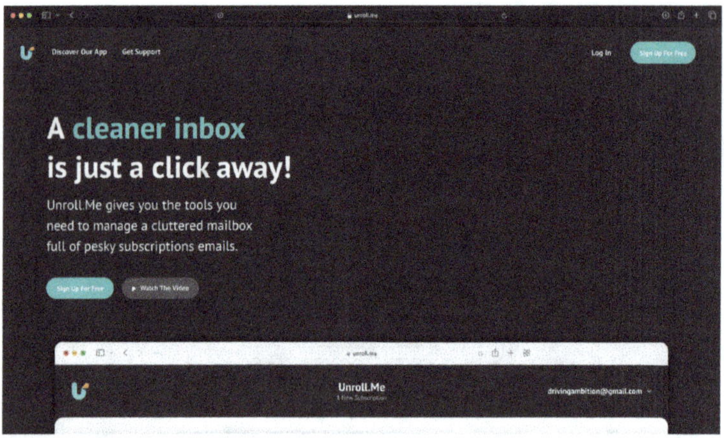

- **How it saves time:** Reduces inbox clutter and manages email subscriptions efficiently.

34. Withinhours.com

- **What it does:** Finds cities within a specific radius for targeted ads.

- **Resource type:** Geolocation tool.

- **Cost:** Free.

- **How it saves time:** Enables quick geotargeting for location-specific ad campaigns.

35. 2short.ai

- **What it does:** Converts YouTube videos into short clips with captions.

- **Resource type:** Video editing automation tool.

- **Cost:** Free.

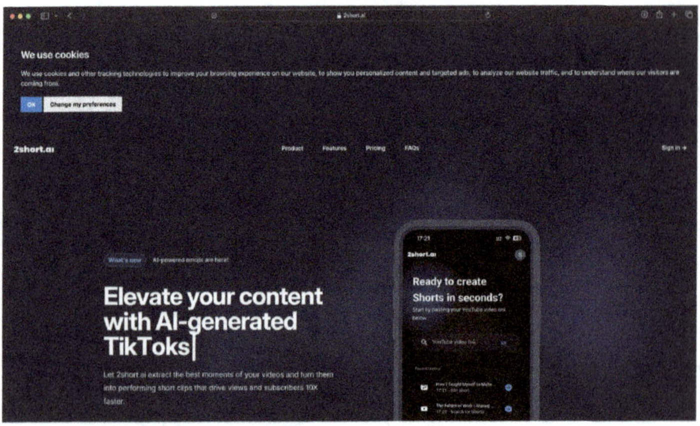

- **How it saves time:** Simplifies the creation of short, engaging content for platforms like TikTok or Instagram.

36. Snackprompt.com

- **What it does:** Uses ChatGPT to create Instagram post ideas and captions.

- **Resource type:** AI-powered content ideation tool.

- **Cost:** Free.

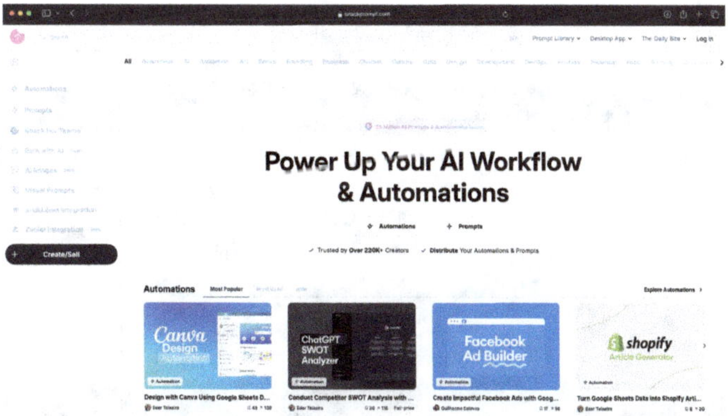

- **How it saves time:** Quickly generates creative ideas, saving time on brainstorming sessions.

37. Heygen.com

- **What it does:** Allows users to create personalized AI avatars for videos.

- **Resource type:** AI avatar generator.

- **Cost:** Free and paid options.

- **How it saves time:** Automates avatar creation, eliminating the need for live video recording.

38. Durable.co

- **What it does:** A website builder designed for small businesses.

- **Resource type:** Website creation platform.

- **Cost:** Paid.

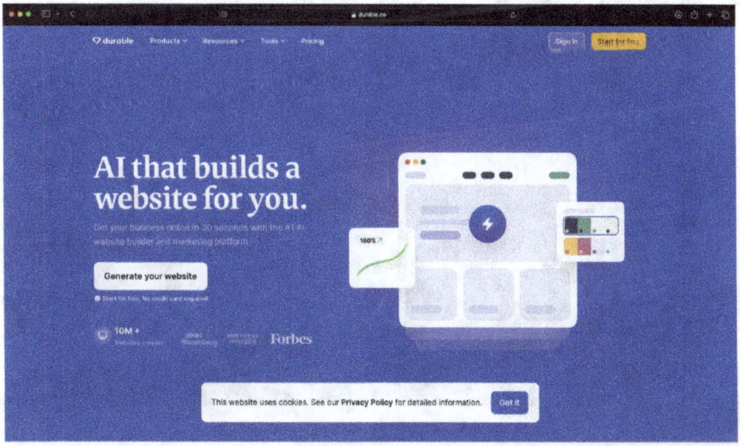

- **How it saves time:** Provides a quick setup for creating professional websites without coding.

39. Flutterflow.io

- **What it does:** A platform for building custom mobile apps.

- **Resource type:** App development tool.

- **Cost:** Paid.

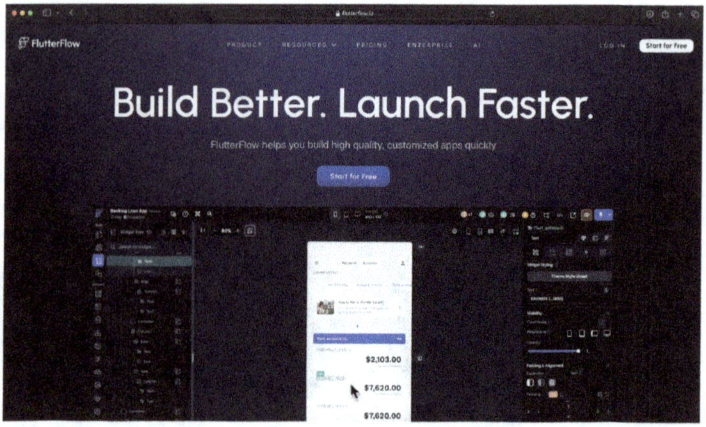

- **How it saves time:** Simplifies app creation with drag-and-drop functionality.

40. Kaiber.ai

- **What it does:** AI tool for creating animated videos.

- **Resource type:** Animation and video production platform.

- **Cost:** Paid.

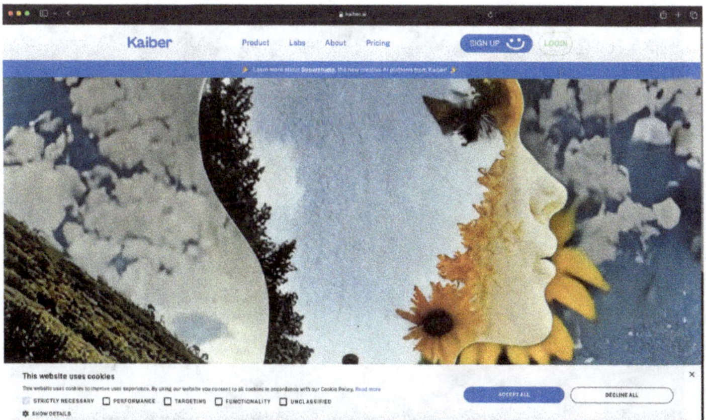

- **How it saves time:** Streamlines animation processes, enabling quick content production.

41. Tome.app

- **What it does:** AI-powered platform for creating visually engaging presentations.

- **Resource type:** Presentation tool.

- **Cost:** Free.

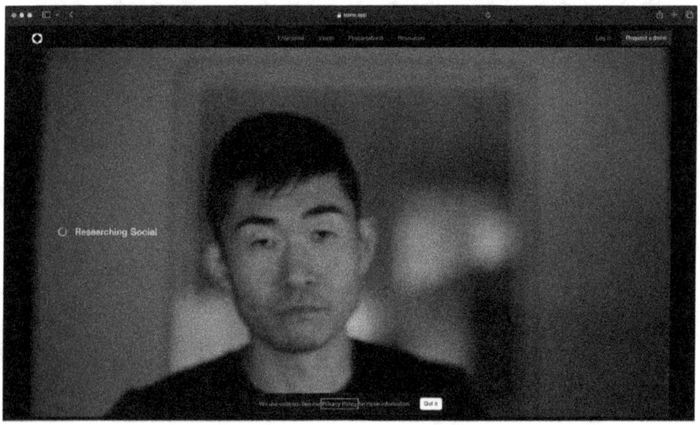

- **How it saves time:** Automates the design process, allowing creators to focus on content.

42. Contlo.com

- **What it does:** Provides AI-driven marketing tools for content creation and customer engagement.

- **Resource type:** Marketing automation platform.

- **Cost:** Free and paid plans.

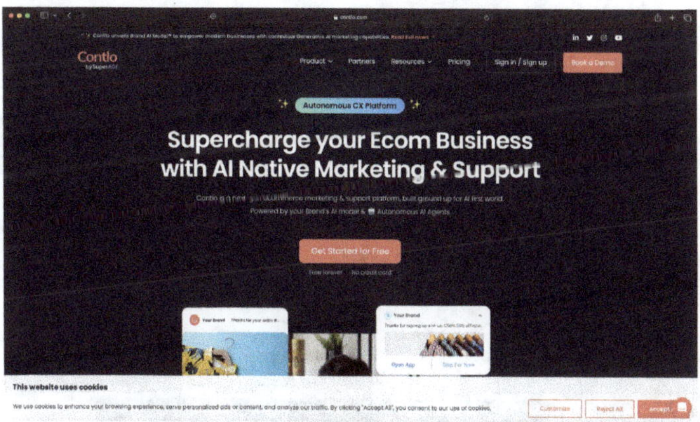

- **How it saves time:** Automates marketing tasks, freeing up time for strategic planning.

43. Simplified.com

- **What it does:** Offers tools for graphic design, content scheduling, and social media management.

- **Resource type:** Social media management tool.

- **Cost:** Free and paid plans.

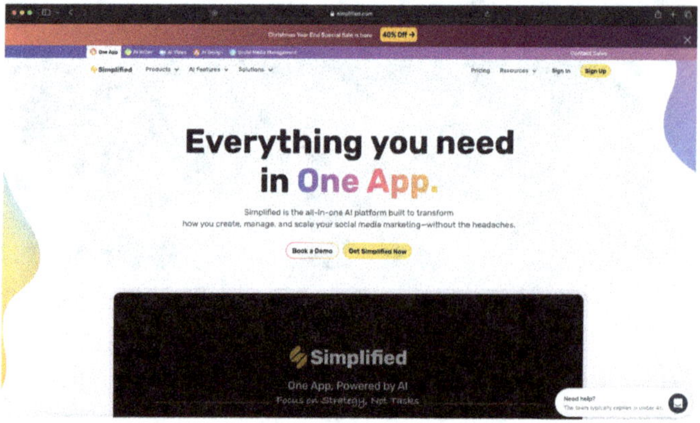

- **How it saves time:** Combines multiple social media tools in one platform, streamlining workflows.

44. Logicballs.com

- **What it does:** AI-powered ad writer and marketing tool.

- **Resource type:** Ad generation platform.

- **Cost:** Free and paid plans.

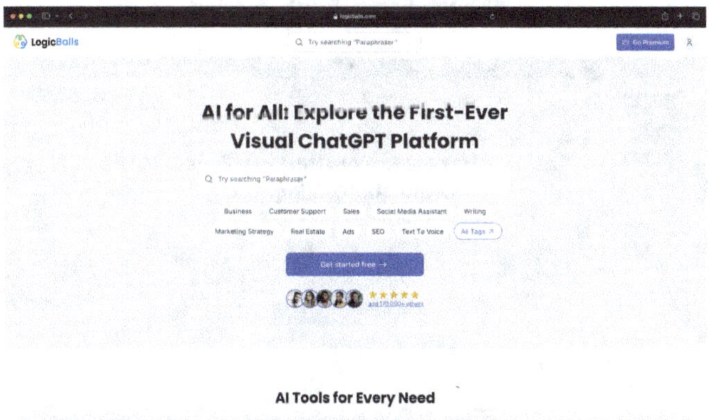

- **How it saves time:** Automates the creation of effective ad copy, reducing time spent on drafting.

45. Boords.com

- **What it does:** Creates AI-generated illustrations and storyboards for visual projects.

- **Resource type:** Illustration and design platform.

- **Cost:** Free and paid options.

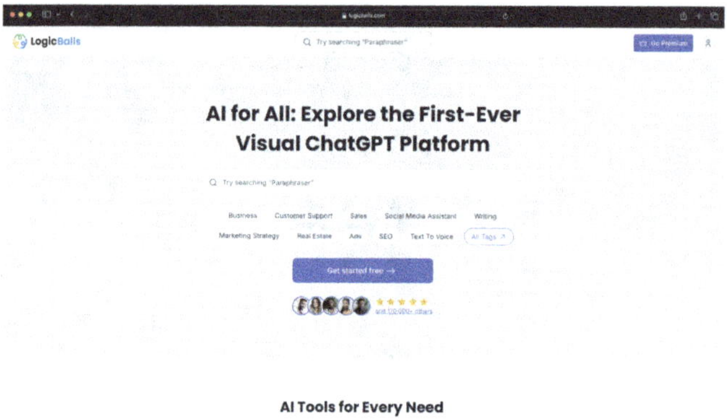

- **How it saves time:** Automates storyboard creation, providing quick visuals for pre-production.

46. FrameSet.app

- **What it does:** Provides stock photos optimized for color grading.

- **Resource type:** Stock photo platform.

- **Cost:** Free.

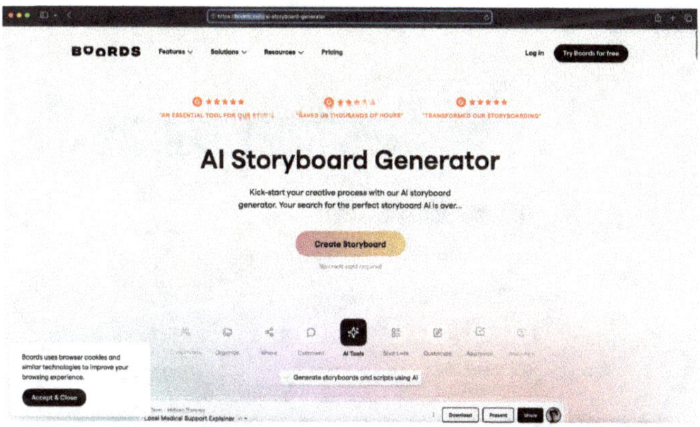

- **How it saves time:** Offers ready-to-use stock images, saving time on image sourcing and editing.

47. Mindluster.com

- **What it does:** Provides free online courses in various fields.

- **Resource type:** E-learning platform.

- **Cost:** Free.

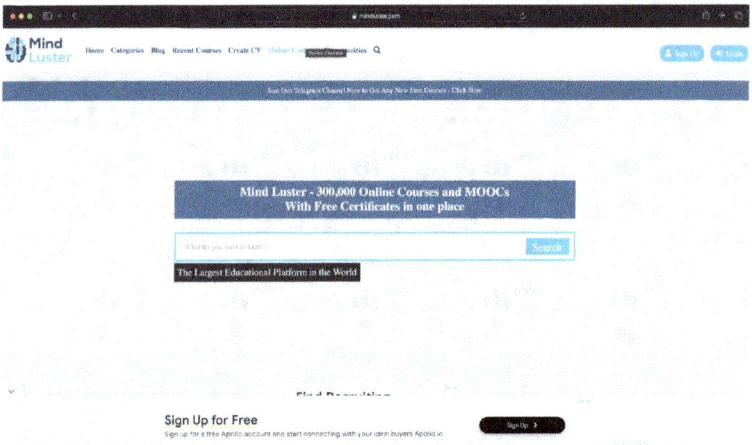

- **How it saves time:** Offers accessible learning materials to enhance skills without additional cost.

48. Mixkit.co

- **What it does:** Offers free music, video, and image resources for creators.

- **Resource type:** Stock media platform.

- **Cost:** Free.

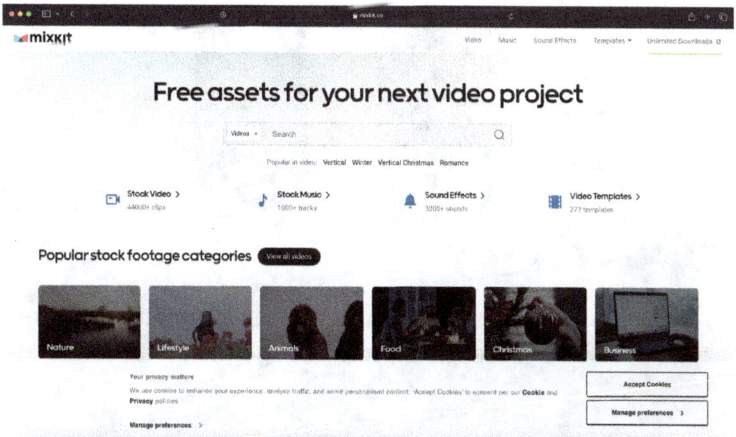

- **How it saves time:** Provides instant access to creative assets, reducing production time.

49. Submagic.co

- **What it does:** Creates advanced captions for videos.

- **Resource type:** Captioning tool.

- **Cost:** Paid.

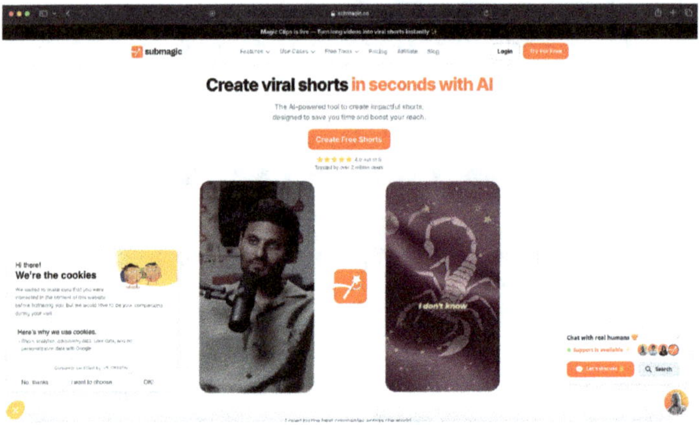

- **How it saves time:** Automates caption generation, ensuring accessibility and engagement.

50. Cheatlayer.com

- **What it does:** Automates tasks and content posting for social media.

- **Resource type:** Social media automation tool.

- **Cost:** Paid.

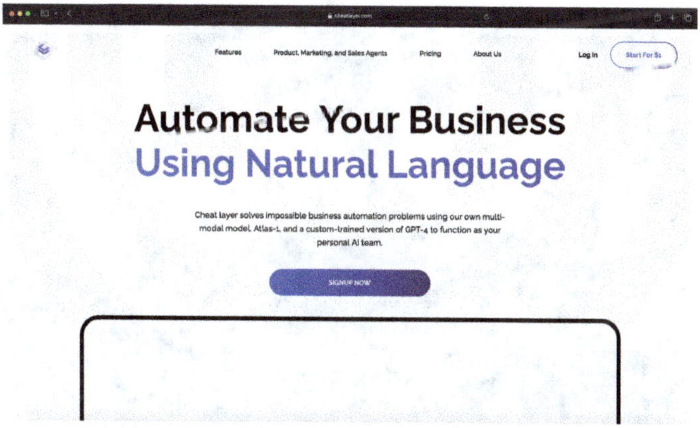

- **How it saves time:** Automates repetitive tasks like scheduling and posting, freeing time for strategy.

51. Recraft.ai

- **What it does:** Generates AI-powered illustrations for branding and design.

- **Resource type:** Illustration tool.

- **Cost:** Free and paid plans.

- **How it saves time:** Quickly produces illustrations for branding without hiring a designer.

52. Syllaby.io

- **What it does:** AI-driven platform for content creation, including scripts, blogs, and video ideas.

- **Resource type:** Content ideation tool.

- **Cost:** Paid.

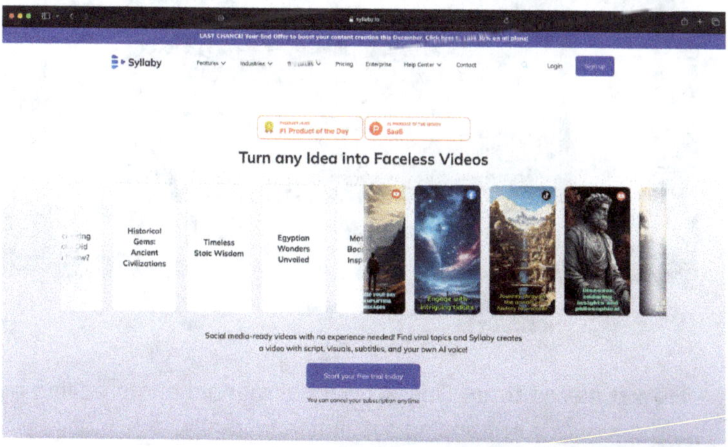

- **How it saves time:** Automates script and content creation, reducing brainstorming time.

53. ImgLarger.com

- **What it does:** Upscales images without losing quality.

- **Resource type**: Image enhancement tool.

- **Cost:** Free and paid plans.

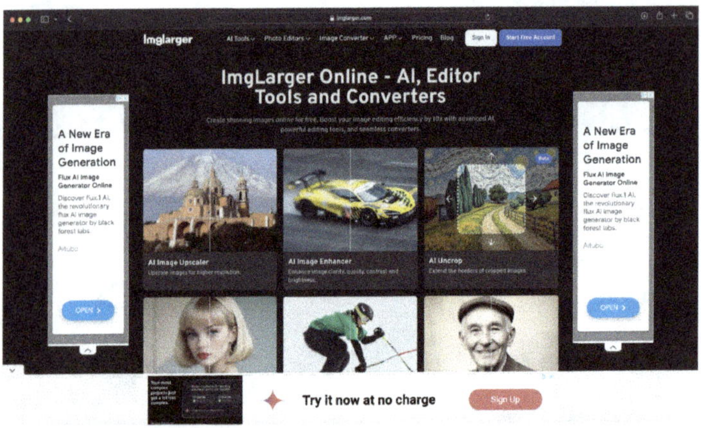

- **How it saves time:** Saves hours of manual photo editing by enhancing resolution instantly.

54. VisMe.co

- **What it does:** Creates animated forms and visual storytelling experiences.

- **Resource type:** Animation and storytelling tool.

- **Cost:** Free and paid plans.

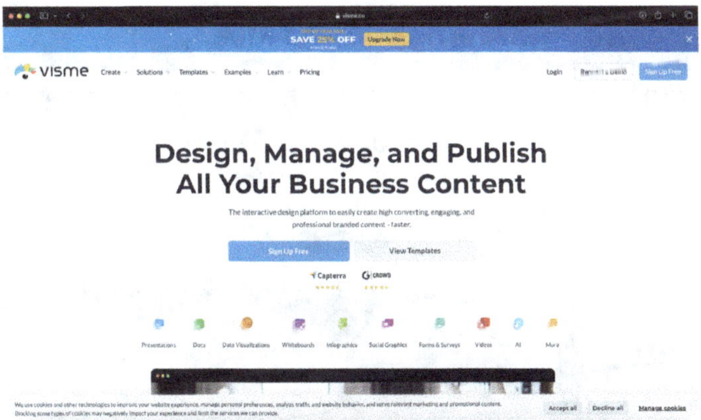

- **How it saves time:** Automates animations, enabling creators to focus on storytelling.

55. Heygen AI

- **What it does:** Translates videos into multiple languages using AI.

- **Resource type:** AI translation tool.

- **Cost:** Free and paid plans.

- **How it saves time:** Automates translations, enabling global reach without manual efforts.

56. Make.com

- **What it does:** Automates workflows and connects various apps.

- **Resource type:** Workflow automation tool.

- **Cost:** Paid.

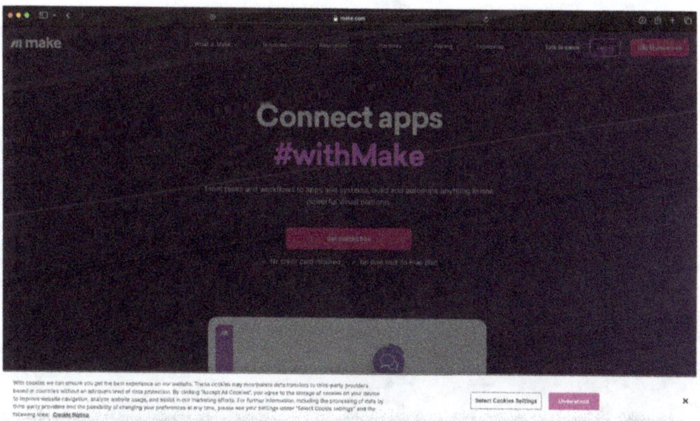

- **How it saves time:** Integrates apps to streamline workflows, eliminating manual data transfers.

57. Framer.io

- **What it does:** AI-powered website creation and design tool.

- **Resource type:** Website builder.

- **Cost:** Free and paid plans.

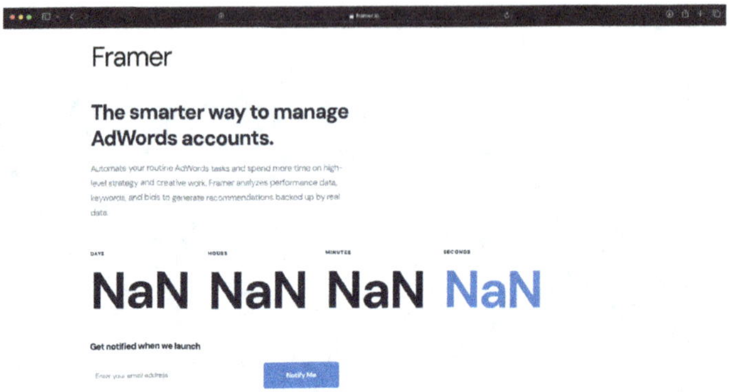

- **How it saves time:** Automates website creation with easy drag-and-drop functionality.

58. Visla.us

- **What it does:** Converts text into videos, allowing creators to produce explainer content effortlessly.

- **Resource type:** Video creation platform.

- **Cost:** Free.

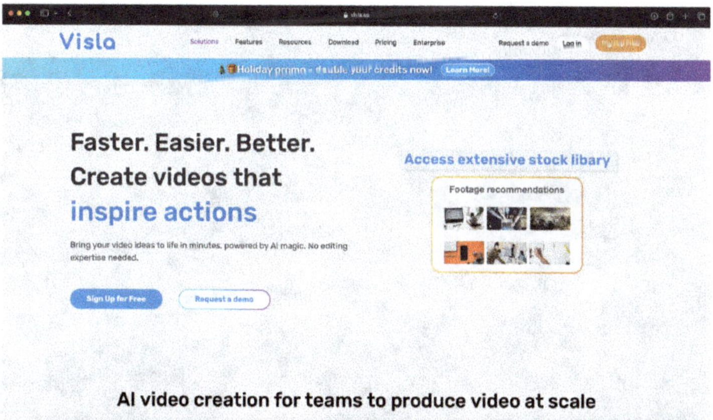

- **How it saves time:** Automates video production from textual content, reducing editing time.

59. Opus.pro

- **What it does:** Creates short-form video content with captions and SEO optimization.

- **Resource type:** Video editing tool.

- **Cost:** Free.

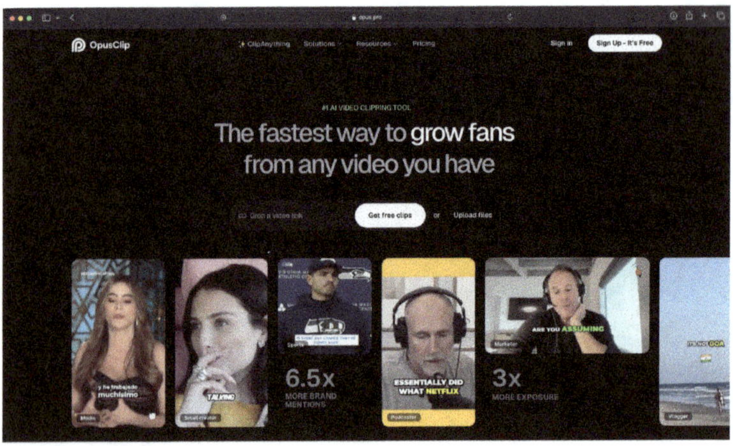

- **How it saves time:** Automates SEO and video editing processes, enabling rapid content production.

60. Space Type Generator

- **What it does:** Creates unique typography for branding and design projects.

- **Resource type:** Typography tool.

- **Cost:** Free.

- **How it saves time:** Provides customizable typographic designs, simplifying branding workflows.

61. Alternativeto.net

- **What it does:** Suggests alternative software and tools for specific needs.

- **Resource type:** Research platform.

- **Cost:** Free.

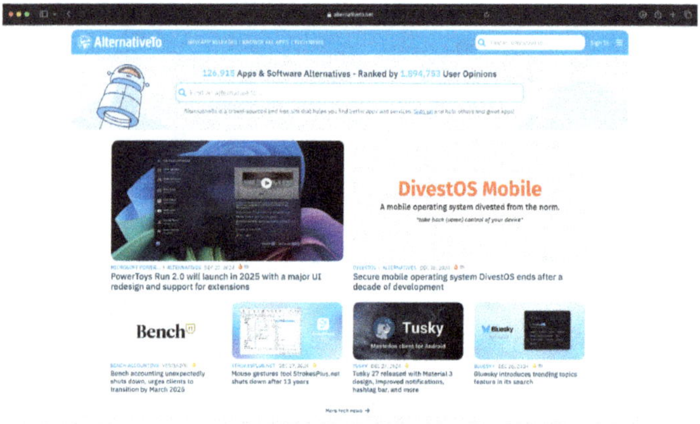

- **How it saves time:** Quickly identifies substitute tools to enhance workflows.

62. Hyperwrite.ai

- **What it does:** AI-powered tool for creative writing and idea generation.

- **Resource type:** Writing automation platform.

- **Cost:** Free and paid plans.

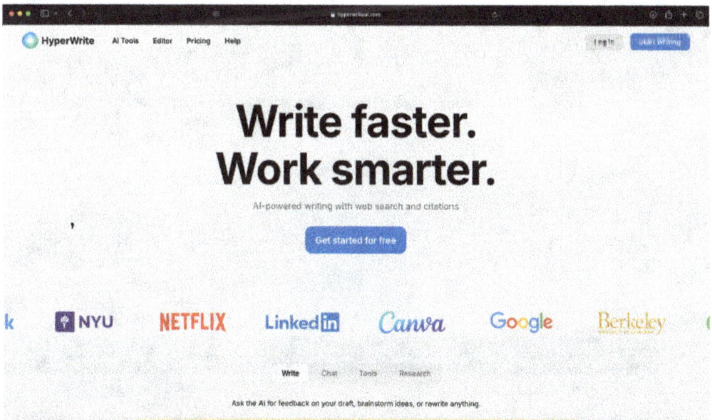

- **How it saves time:** Generates content ideas and drafts, saving hours of writing.

63. Aiter.io

- **What it does:** Analyzes website URLs and provides AI-driven marketing insights.

- **Resource type:** Marketing analysis tool.

- **Cost:** Free and paid plans.

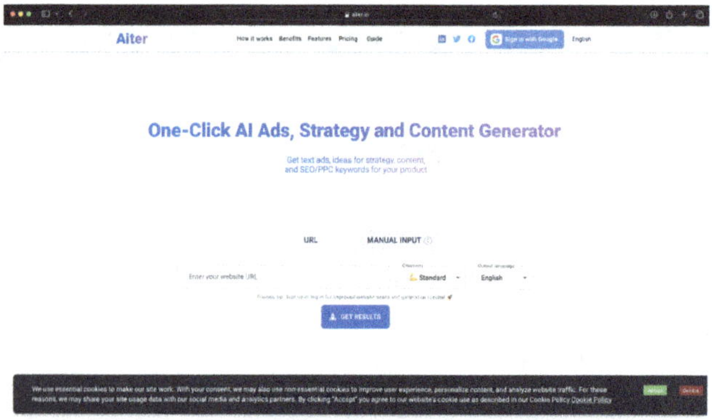

- **How it saves time:** Offers automated insights, eliminating manual data analysis.

64. Filepizza.com

- **What it does:** Peer-to-peer file-sharing tool without requiring uploads to servers.

- **Resource type:** File transfer platform.

- **Cost:** Free.

- **How it saves time:** Enables instant file sharing without lengthy uploads or downloads.

65. Notion.com

- **What it does:** All-in-one productivity tool for managing tasks, notes, databases, and collaboration.

- **Resource type:** Workspace and project management tool.

- **Cost:** Free tier; premium plans for teams.

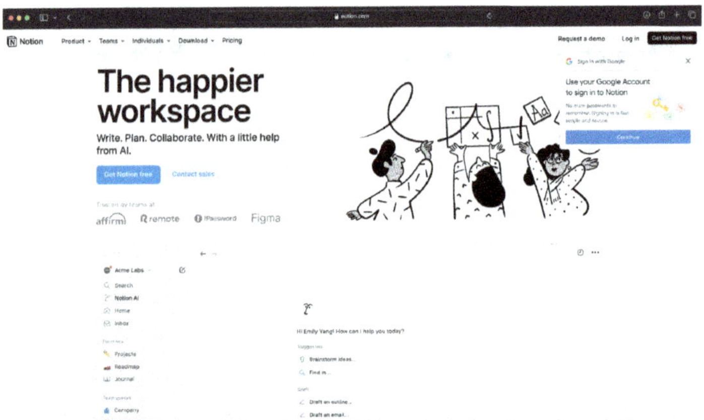

- **How it saves time:** Centralizes multiple tools into one, reducing the need for switching between platforms.

66. Onlineconvert.com

- **What it does:** Converts files between different formats (e.g., audio, video, and documents).

- **Resource type:** File conversion tool.

- **Cost:** Free with limitations; paid plans for advanced features.

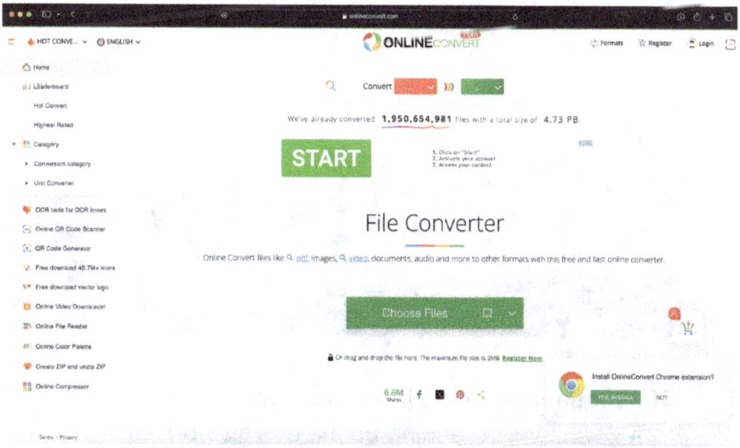

- **How it saves time:** Speeds up the conversion process, eliminating the need for specialized software.

67. 0to255.com

- **What it does:** Simplifies the process of finding color variations for web and graphic design.

- **Resource type:** Color design tool.

- **Cost:** Free.

- **How it saves time:** Quickly generates color palettes and shades, speeding up the design workflow.

68. Blisk.io

- **What it does:** Provides a browser designed for developers to test websites across multiple devices simultaneously.

- **Resource type:** Development and testing tool.

- **Cost:** Paid.

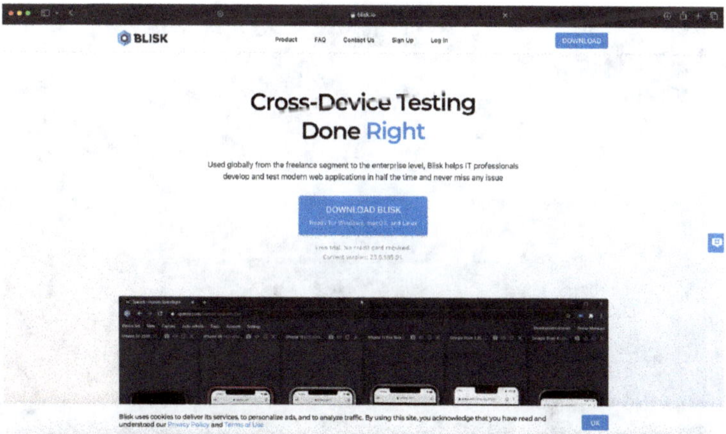

- **How it saves time:** Simplifies testing processes by allowing simultaneous testing on various device formats.

69. Leonardo.ai

- **What it does:** AI-powered platform for generating high-quality art and illustrations.

- **Resource type:** Illustration creation tool.

- **Cost:** Free and paid options.

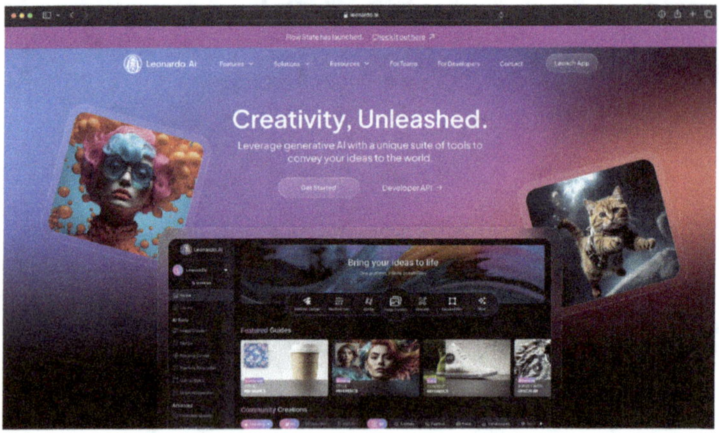

- **How it saves time:** Allows creators to generate artwork instantly, eliminating manual drawing processes.

70. Uizard.io

- **What it does:** Generates user interface designs from text descriptions.

- **Resource type:** UI/UX design tool.

- **Cost:** Free and paid options.

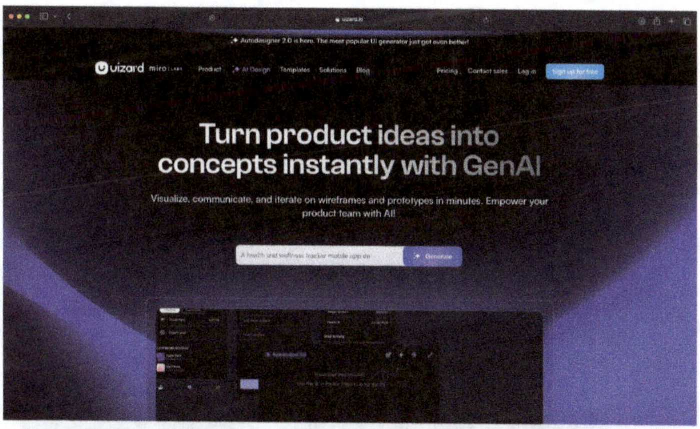

- **How it saves time:** Quickly transforms ideas into professional UI/UX designs without advanced design skills.

71. ContentIdeas.io

- **What it does:** Generates content ideas based on trending topics and keywords.

- **Resource type:** Content ideation tool.

- **Cost:** Free.

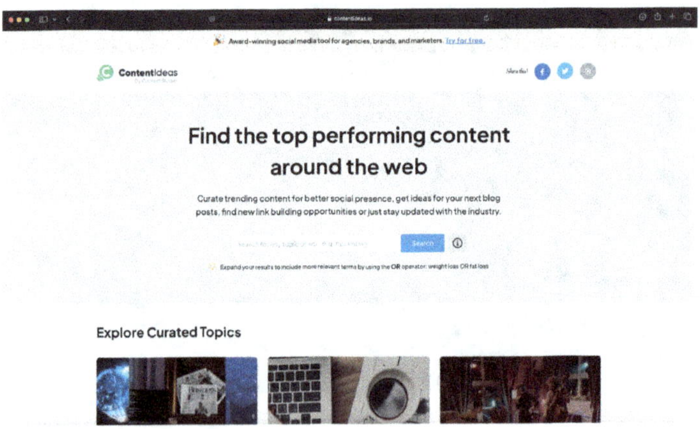

- **How it saves time:** Provides ready-to-use content ideas, minimizing brainstorming efforts.

72. Mocky.ai

- **What it does:** Offers mockup tools for designing and testing web apps and platforms.

- **Resource type:** Prototyping tool.

- **Cost:** Free.

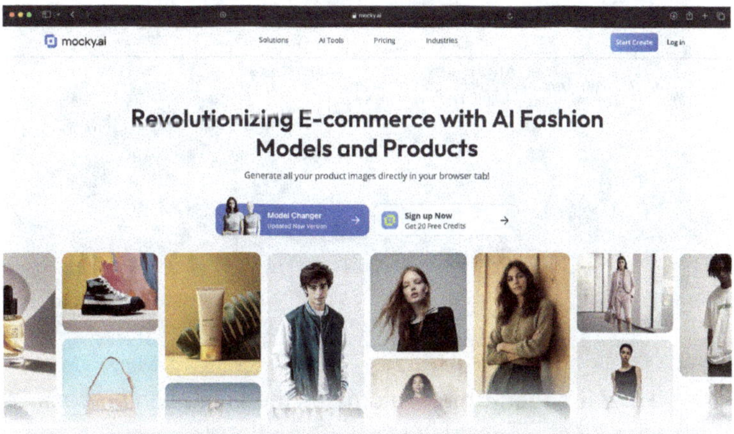

- **How it saves time:** Simplifies the testing phase by generating realistic mockups quickly.

73. Steve.ai

- **What it does:** Turns text into animated videos quickly.

- **Resource type:** Video creation platform.

- **Cost:** Paid.

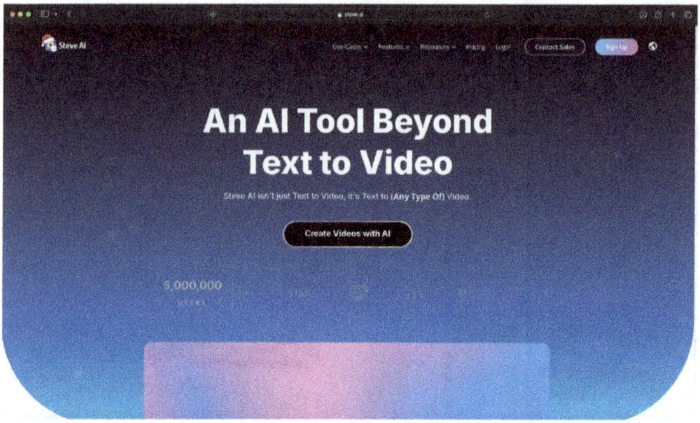

- **How it saves time:** Automates the animation process, saving hours of manual work.

74. Autodraw.com

- **What it does:** Converts rough sketches into polished drawings using AI.

- **Resource type:** Drawing enhancement tool.

- **Cost:** Free.

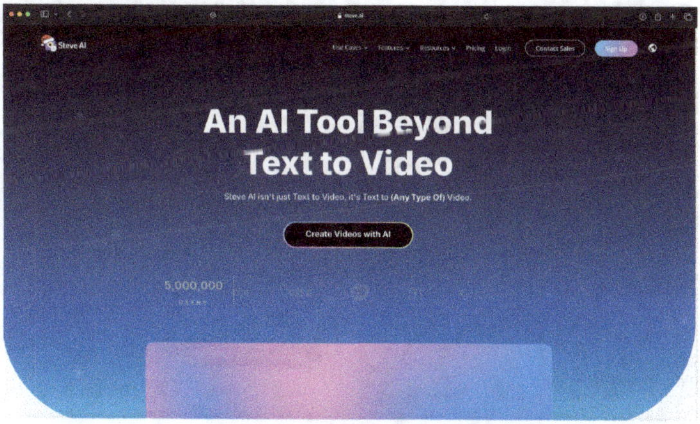

- **How it saves time:** Provides professional-looking drawings instantly from rough sketches.

75. Cohesive.so

- **What it does:** AI-powered script and content generator for blogs, ads, and video ideas.

- **Resource type:** Writing and content creation tool.

- **Cost:** Free.

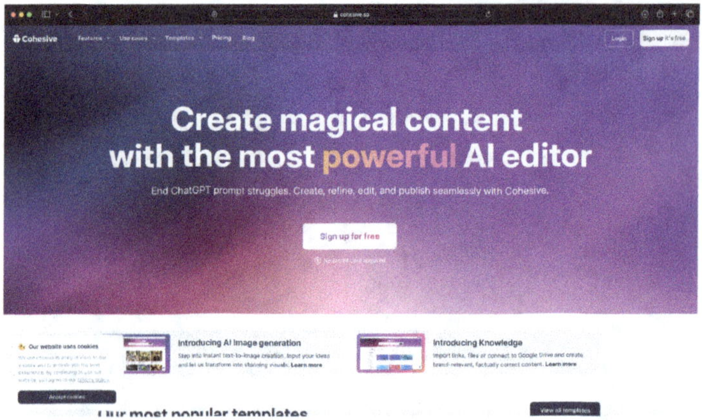

- **How it saves time:** Reduces content creation time with pre-generated scripts and posts.

76. Zmo.ai

- **What it does:** Offers AI-generated fashion models for use in marketing campaigns.

- **Resource type:** AI modeling platform.

- **Cost:** Free and paid plans.

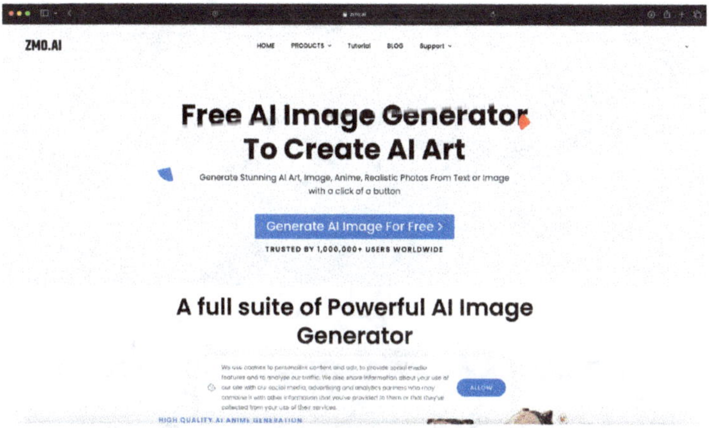

- **How it saves time:** Eliminates the need for photo shoots by generating models digitally.

77. Marketsy.ai

- **What it does:** AI-driven tool for creating and managing online stores.

- **Resource type:** E-commerce platform.

- **Cost:** Paid.

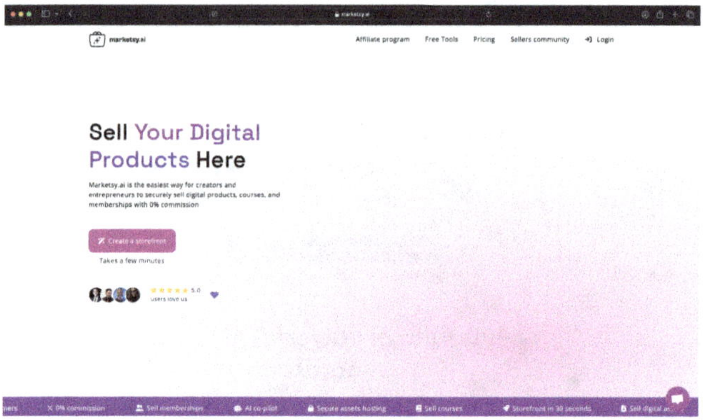

- **How it saves time:** Automates e-commerce setup and management, saving hours of backend work.

78. TextCortex.ai

- **What it does:** AI-powered tool for automating text creation, including emails, ads, and blogs.

- **Resource type:** Content automation tool.

- **Cost:** Free and paid.

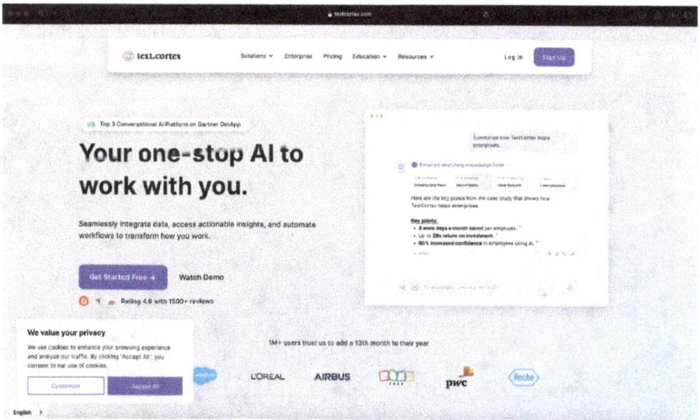

- **How it saves time:** Reduces time spent drafting content by providing AI-generated suggestions.

79.RunwayML.com

- **What it does:** Provides AI tools for creating and editing videos, images, and text-to-image models.

- **Resource type:** Creative content generation platform.

- **Cost:** Free tier available; paid plans for advanced features.

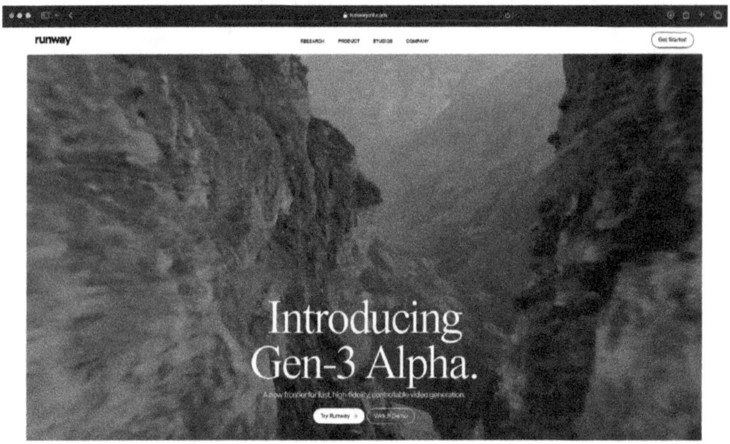

- **How it saves time:** Automates creative processes like background removal, object recognition, and video editing.

80. Descript.com

- **What it does:** Combines audio and video editing with transcription and screen recording.

- **Resource type:** Media editing tool.

- **Cost:** Free with limitations; premium plans available.

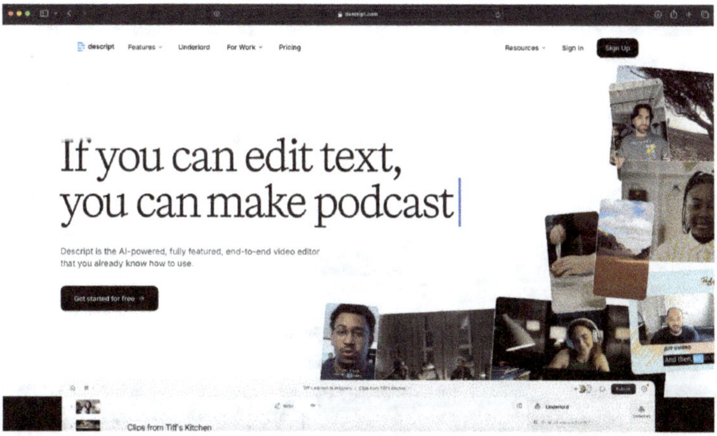

- **How it saves time:** Simplifies editing by allowing creators to edit video and audio as if they were editing text.

81. Lumen5.com

- **What it does:** Converts blog posts and articles into engaging videos.

- **Resource type:** Video creation tool.

- **Cost:** Free and paid plans.

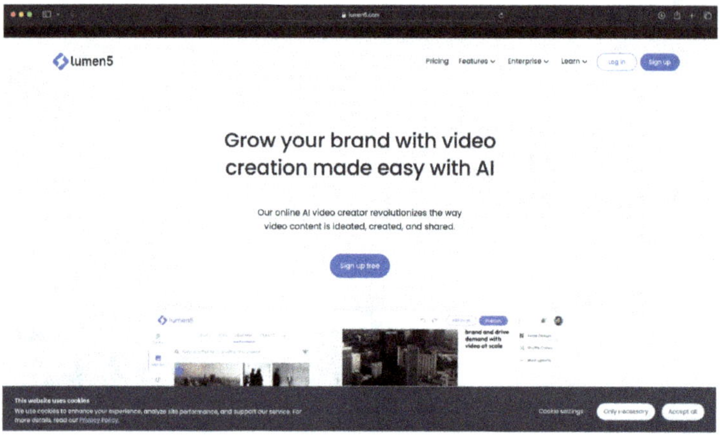

- **How it saves time:** Automates video production using AI, transforming written content into videos with minimal effort.

82. Camtasia.com

- **What it does:** Screen recording and video editing software for tutorials and presentations.

- **Resource type:** Video editing tool.

- **Cost:** Paid.

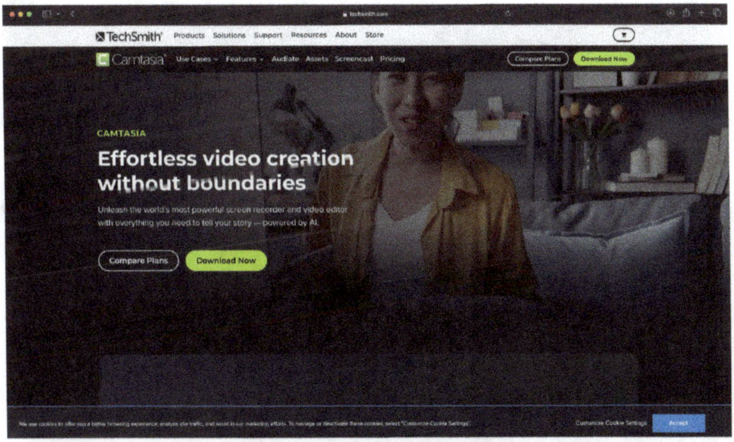

- **How it saves time:** Provides a user-friendly interface for creating polished video tutorials quickly.

83. Figma.com

- **What it does:** Collaborative design tool for creating UI/UX prototypes and mockups.

- **Resource type:** Design platform.

- **Cost:** Free tier available; premium plans for teams.

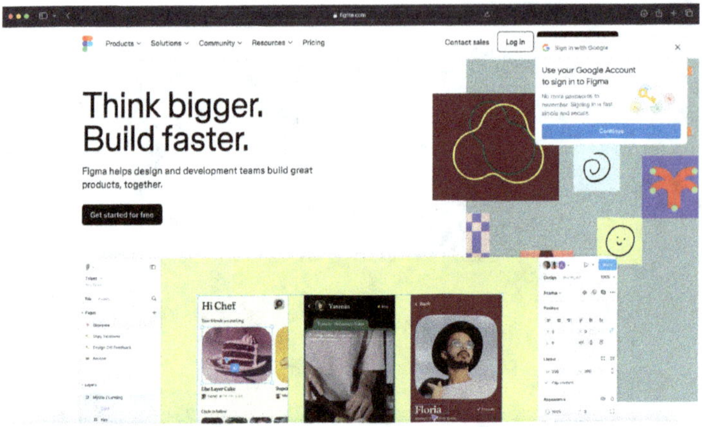

- **How it saves time:** Enables real-time collaboration, reducing back-and-forth in design iterations.

84. Pictory.ai

- **What it does:** Transforms long-form content into short, shareable videos.

- **Resource type:** Video summarization tool.

- **Cost:** Paid.

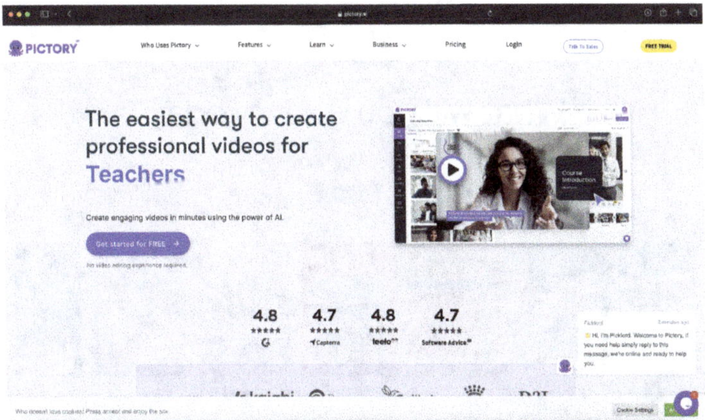

- **How it saves time:** Automates video creation from scripts, blogs, or articles, reducing manual editing.

85. Canva.com

- **What it does:** Graphic design platform with templates for social media posts, presentations, and more.

- **Resource type:** Design tool.

- **Cost:** Free and paid options.

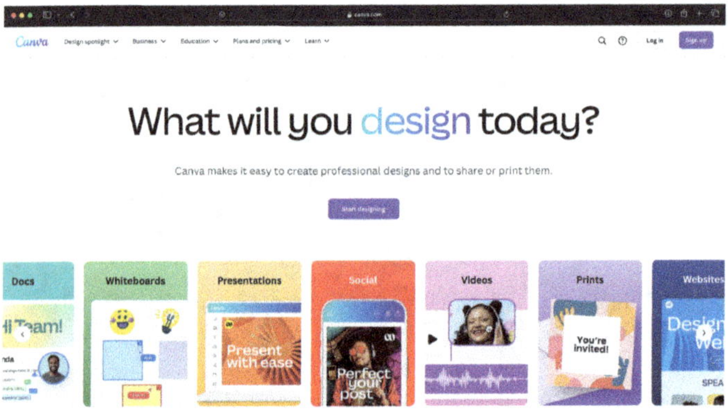

- **How it saves time:** Offers ready-to-use templates for fast design creation.

86. Kapwing.com

- **What it does:** Online video editor for resizing, subtitling, and meme creation.

- **Resource type:** Video editing tool.

- **Cost:** Free and paid plans

- **How it saves time:** Provides quick editing tools tailored to social media platforms.

87. Audiio.com

- **What it does:** Offers a library of royalty-free music for video creators.

- **Resource type:** Audio licensing platform.

- **Cost:** Paid.

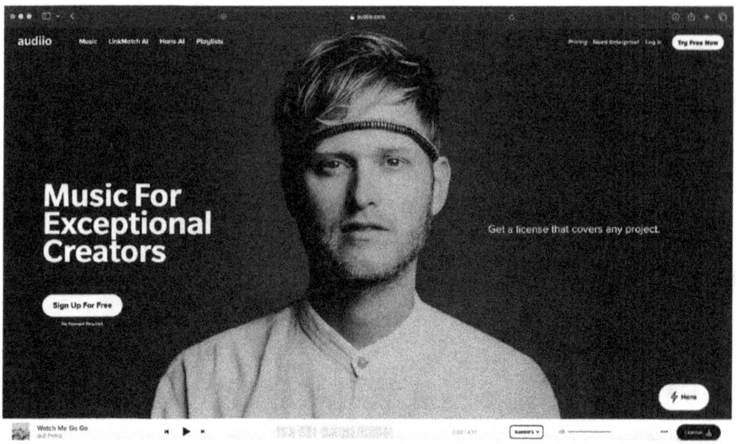

- **How it saves time:** Simplifies music licensing, allowing creators to focus on production.

88. ClickUp.com

- **What it does:** Project management tool combining tasks, docs, and timelines.

- **Resource type:** Productivity platform.

- **Cost:** Free and paid options.

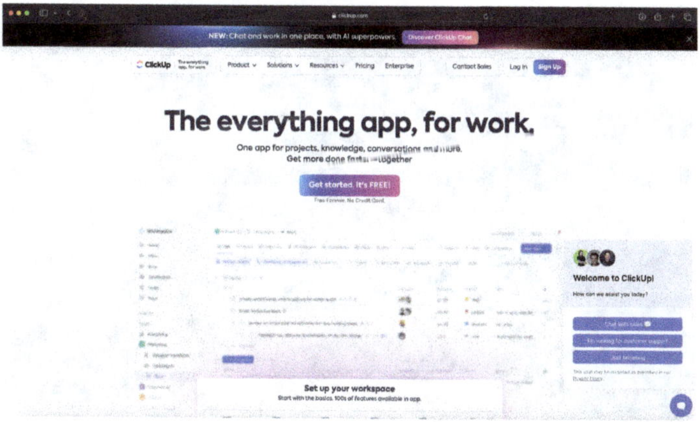

- **How it saves time:** Integrates multiple productivity tools into one platform.

89. Tella.tv

- **What it does:** Enables screen recording and editing for creating tutorials and presentations.

- **Resource type:** Video recording tool.

- **Cost:** Paid.

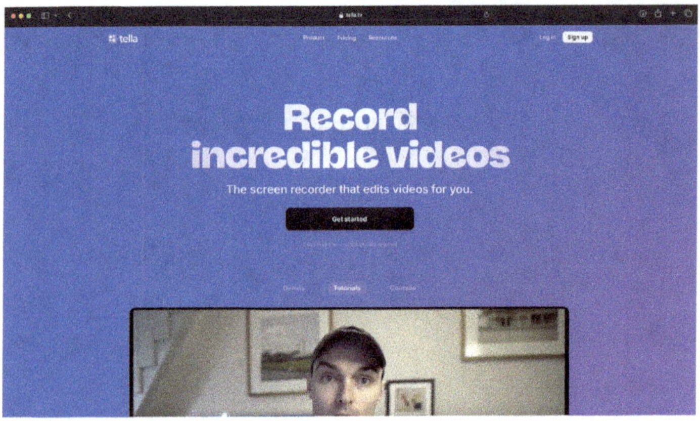

- **How it saves time:** Streamlines the process of creating polished educational videos.

90. Plask.ai

- **What it does:** AI-powered motion capture and animation tool.

- **Resource type:** Animation platform.

- **Cost:** Paid.

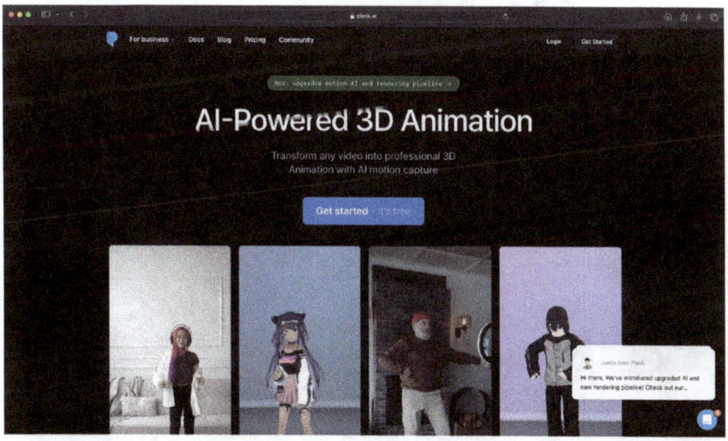

- **How it saves time:** Automates motion capture for realistic animations.

91. Jasper.ai

- **What it does:** AI writing assistant for creating blog posts, ads, and social media content.

- **Resource type:** Content creation platform.

- **Cost:** Paid.

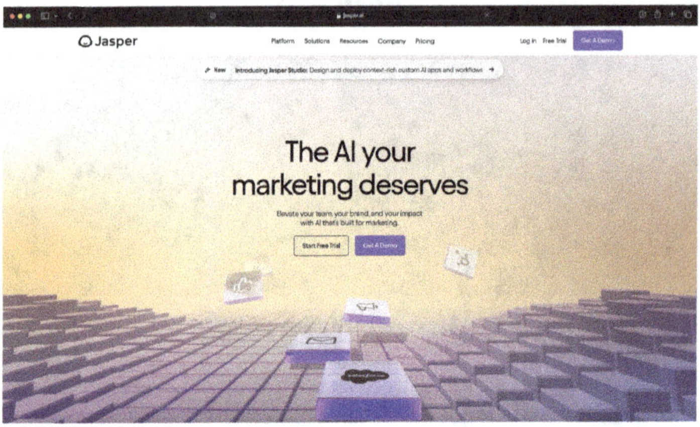

- **How it saves time:** Automates writing tasks, reducing brainstorming and drafting time.

92. Frame.io

- **What it does:** Collaboration tool for video editing teams to provide feedback and revisions.

- **Resource type:** Review and collaboration platform.

- **Cost:** Paid.

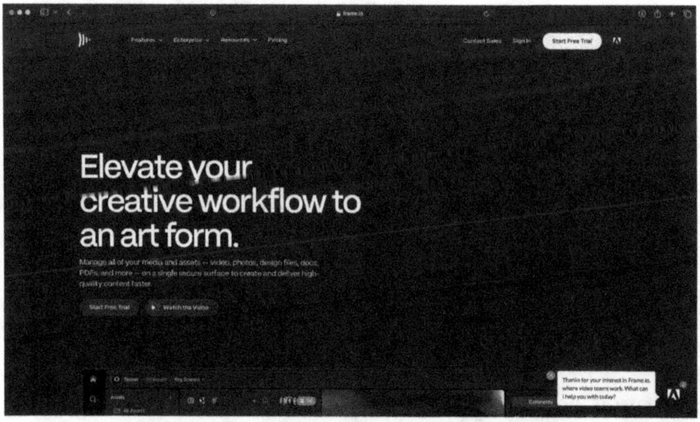

- **How it saves time:** Centralizes feedback, streamlining the editing process.

93. Otter.ai

- What it does: Transcribes audio and video into editable text.

- Resource type: Transcription tool.

- Cost: Free and paid plans.

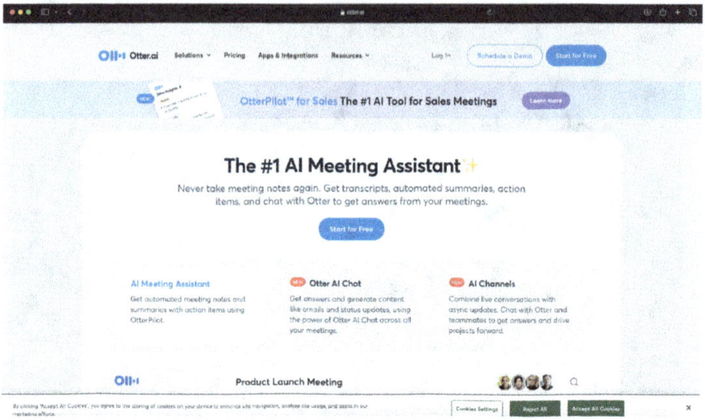

- How it saves time: Automates transcription, eliminating manual typing.

94. Grammarly.com

- **What it does:** Writing assistant that checks grammar, spelling, and style.

- **Resource type:** Editing tool.

- **Cost:** Free and paid plans.

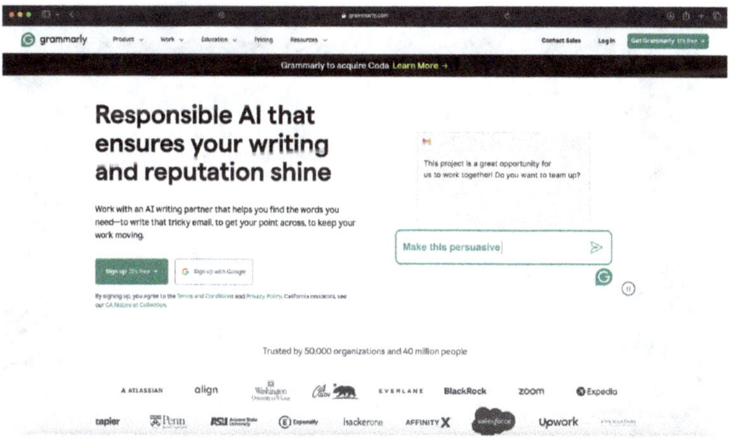

- **How it saves time:** Improves content quality without the need for manual proofreading.

95. Lalal.ai

- **What it does:** AI-powered tool for isolating vocals and instruments in audio tracks.

- **Resource type:** Audio editing platform.

- **Cost:** Paid.

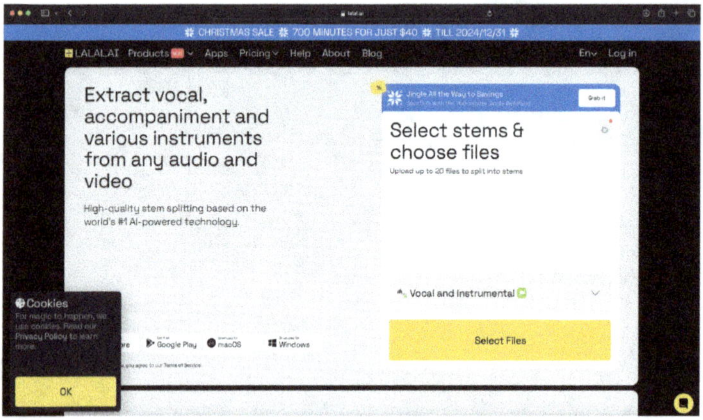

- **How it saves time:** Automates stem extraction, streamlining music editing.

96. Bitly.com

What it does: URL shortening and link tracking service.

- **Resource type:** Marketing tool.

- **Cost:** Free and paid options.

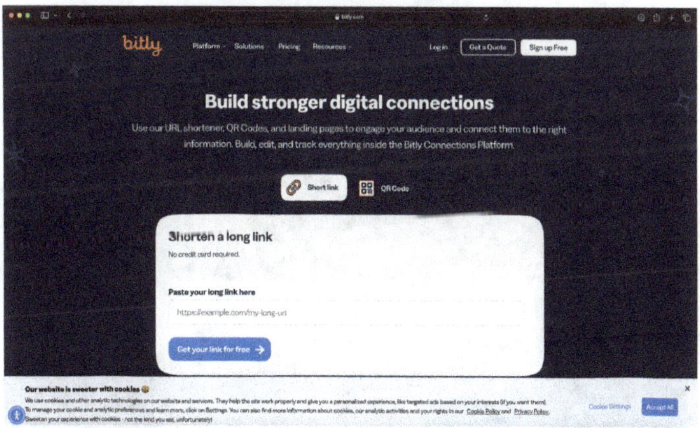

- **How it saves time:** Simplifies link management for campaigns.

97. Animoto.com

- **What it does:** Creates professional videos from templates and user-provided media.

- **Resource type:** Video creation tool.

- **Cost:** Paid.

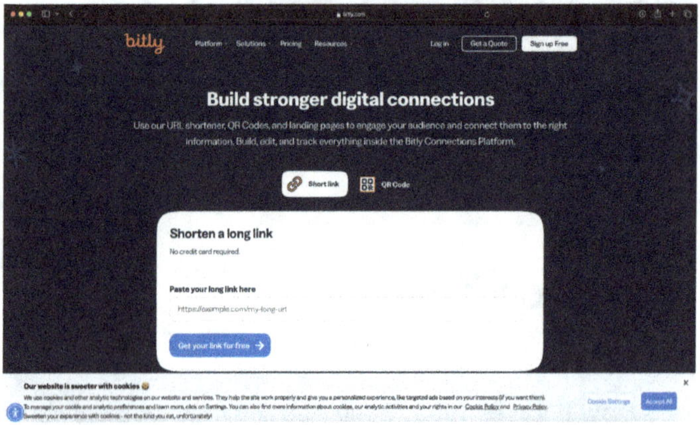

- **How it saves time:** Reduces video editing complexity with drag-and-drop functionality.

98. VistaCreate.com

- **What it does:** Design tool for creating marketing materials and social media content.

- **Resource type:** Graphic design platform.

- **Cost:** Free and paid plans.

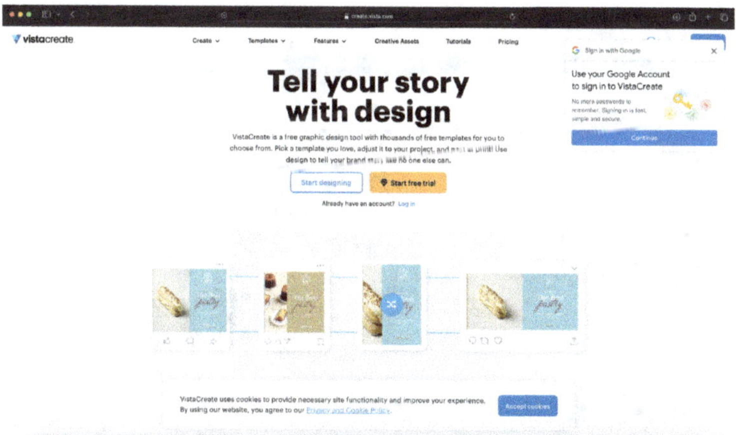

- **How it saves time:** Offers a vast template library for quick design creation.

99. CoSchedule.com

- **What it does:** Social media scheduling and marketing calendar platform.

- **Resource type:** Marketing management tool.

- **Cost:** Paid.

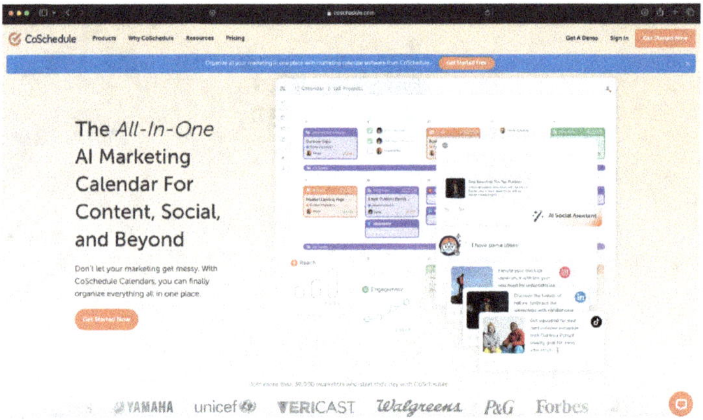

- **How it saves time:** Centralizes social media management and analytics in one platform.

100. Clipscribe.com

- **What it does:** Adds captions, headlines, and progress bars to social media videos.

- **Resource type:** Video editing tool.

- **Cost:** Paid.

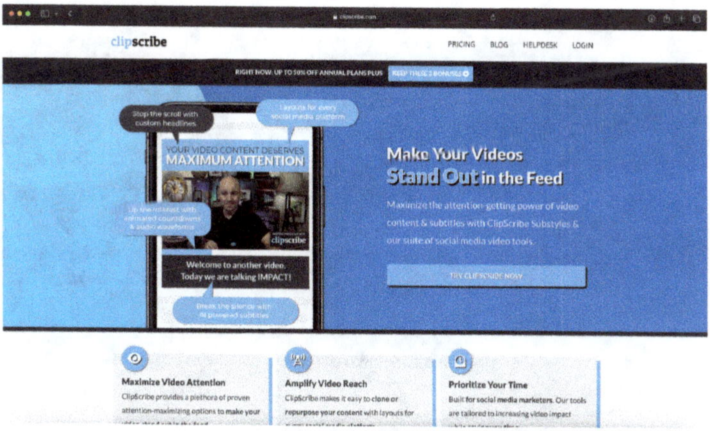

- **How it saves time:** Enhances video content for better engagement with minimal effort.

101. Movavi.com

- **What it does:** Video editing software for beginners and professionals.

- **Resource type:** Video editing platform.

- **Cost:** Paid.

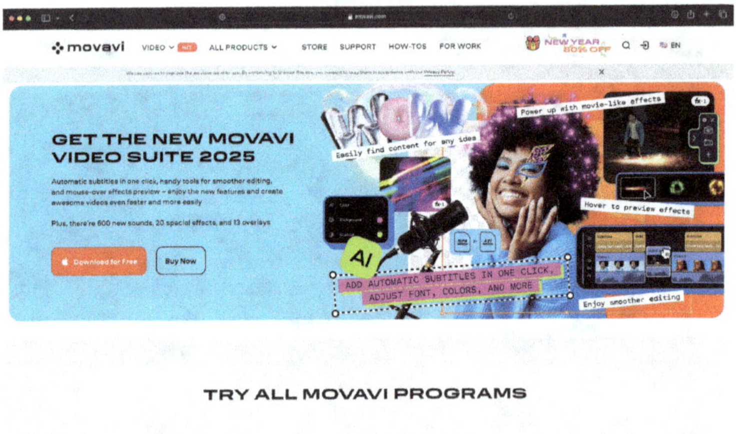

- **How it saves time:** Provides intuitive editing features that streamline content creation.

102. Webflow.com

- **What it does:** Website builder that combines visual design with robust CMS tools.

- **Resource type:** Website creation platform.

- **Cost:** Paid.

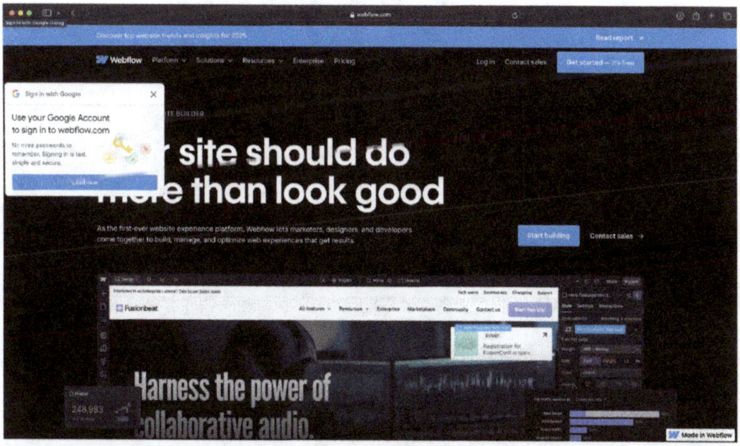

- **How it saves time:** Eliminates the need for coding, allowing creators to focus on design and functionality.

www.ingramcontent.com/pod-product-compliance
Lightning Source LLC
La Vergne TN
LVHW020236210926
848481LV00016B/2337
* 9 7 9 8 3 4 8 4 9 6 5 2 4 *